ALSO BY RUSSELL JALBERT:

Financial Success: How to Plan and When [1986; Horizon Publishing]

Giving- Philanthropy for Everyone [2003; Eileen Saccor]

Honey, Where Did Our Money Go? [2001; Horizon Publishing]

RESCUE
YOUR RETIREMENT

RESCUE
YOUR RETIREMENT

HOW TO OVERCOME WALL
STREET'S DECEPTIONS
AND FAILED FINANCIAL
PLANNING STRATEGIES

RUSSELL JALBERT

Published by Advantage, Charleston, South Carolina.
Member of Advantage Media Group.

ADVANTAGE is a registered trademark and the Advantage colophon is a trademark of Advantage Media Group, Inc.

Printed in the United States of America.

ISBN: 978-159932-302-2
LCCN: 2012933997

This publication is designed to provide accurate and authoritative information in regard to the subject matter covered. It is sold with the understanding that the publisher is not engaged in rendering legal, accounting, or other professional services. If legal advice or other expert assistance is required, the services of a competent professional person should be sought.

Advantage Media Group is proud to be a part of the Tree Neutral® program. Tree Neutral offsets the number of trees consumed in the production and printing of this book by taking proactive steps such as planting trees in direct proportion to the number of trees used to print books. To learn more about Tree Neutral, please visit www.treeneutral.com. To learn more about Advantage's commitment to being a responsible steward of the environment, please visit www.advantagefamily.com/green

Advantage Media Group is a leading publisher of business, motivation, and self-help authors. Do you have a manuscript or book idea that you would like to have considered for publication? Please visit www.amgbook.com or call 1.866.775.1696

DEDICATION

To my sister, Judy, and my daughter, Nicole.
Thank you for your gifts of family and love.

You can find me online at www.jalbertfinancial.com

email me at newswire@jalbertfinancial.com

Like Jalbert Financial Group on Facebook

or follow us on twitter @Jalbert_FG

TABLE OF CONTENTS

CHAPTER 1

THE RE-EDUCATION OF A FINANCIAL ADVISOR

For the past 40 years I have been helping individual investors achieve their financial goals. The period just after September 11, 2001, began my journey into a new financial world. Later came the market crash of 2008, as a result of which I became a zealot in my crusade against Wall Street and the conventional wisdom of financial planning.

Let's go back. On that horrific day in 2001, I came to realize that I did not know whether I could do in the future what I had done in the past. I saw that I was in a new world with new threats. I wondered: Could conventional planning concepts in the cause of safety, growth and income still be effective? At that time, I headed one of the most successful financial practices in the country. People looked to me for advice, and they did as I suggested. That is an enormous responsibility, and I took it very seriously. After the 2001 attacks, there were components in the planning equation that had never been there before—and I needed to reevaluate the factors within that equation through diversification, loss prevention, asset allocation and tech portfolios. I became aware that new thinking and new tools would have to be explored.

Throughout 2002, I researched and found alternative plans that afforded complete principal safety from market-loss, yet provided the opportunity for growth. By 2003, I felt comfortable to share my findings with my clients. My question to them was: Would you be willing to give up some of the upside of the market to have no exposure to the down? These new plans were nearly unanimously embraced. I continued on my journey of safe money from 2003 through 2007, occasionally challenged by investors disappointed that they were under performing their friends. What has Jalbert done?

In 2008, my IQ shot up (in my eyes only). My clients saw the huge market crash and their friends being decimated, while their accounts stayed steady. I used the term "tread water" to mean no losses. All gains had been automatically locked in. Their principal was 100 percent safe. That is when I became a zealot for communicating the deceit and myths of Wall Street and pledged to let people know there was an alternative. *You do not have to risk your assets for the opportunity to grow your money.*

For my words to have a powerful meaning, there must be authenticity and reality behind them, not myths. When clients tell me they're about to retire and ask how to set up their assets, I provide an answer. I make a recommendation to them, and then 10 days later, as they're driving down their turnpike, they turn on their radio and hear, "We interrupt this program to bring you a special bulletin" —and again the world is thrown into chaos. The stock market is closing because of a terrorist attack. That individual who is listening has just placed $2 million in my good, safe hands, and then the stock market closes; two weeks later it opens up, and it's down 50 percent, and my client has lost half of his life savings, he's approaching age 60, and there's not a damn thing I can do about it. That's the world I'm now practicing in.

That's why and when I decided I needed to find something different to offer my clients. After studying the market, I discovered hybrid annuities. I researched them all through 2002, and in 2003 I introduced them to my clients. I'm not a theoretician. I've been in the arena with these vehicles since 2003, and to this date we're about 40 percent ahead of the market, and we've never lost a penny. Providing this form of investment has been a way of moving past the myths I've been referring to condemning. With the hybrid annuity, if the market goes up, my clients get a part of those gains. If it goes down, they tread water.

I have an analogy for this important shift in philosophy. I tell people I used to feel that I was standing on a white sand beach. Picture that landscape and pick out a black stone, about a foot wide. I am perched on that black stone, surrounded by the glare of the white sand. You can hear me up and down the beach calling out, "People, please listen—there is an alternative to what you're hearing." And since 2003, when my stone was so small, there has been a change on the landscape. My stone is now good-sized boulder. Things are being understood, and people are hearing my voice of protest and promise. I'm on the radio, explaining this opportunity across the airwaves. My practice has between 500 and 600 active clients, hearing what I say and acting on it. Some $200 million in cash has flowed into these vehicles. As I say, not one penny of it has ever been lost to a market downturn. For the most part, we're ahead of the market, enjoying significant gains. Most of all, my clients are at peace. And it's not about finding the smartest man in the world; it's simply that plans have been designed, and there's a mathematical formula. That is what drives this investment strategy and this investment tool. If there's prosperity and the market moves up, clients gain. If there's difficulty or any event that knocks the market down, our clients' accounts stay at their prior levels—no losses.

I am but a single voice. Wall Street—and the financial planning industry in general—is a propaganda machine and not a source of accurate information. They're working at keeping American retirement investors from knowing the failings of their industry and their planning tenets.

My concern about Wall Street and the financial planning industry is that they have sold financial planning as a science. People just like you and me believe there's great credibility and reliability in their top experts and sophisticated computer models that kick out recommendations, and it's just not so. In reality, most of those plans are produced for only one reason—to sell you on their reliability, to sell you on trusting their plan. Even though you can look at the data, the graphs and the thickness of the report, it has no basis in reality. I can assure you that the only accurate number in most of those projections is the page number.

Wall Street and financial planners are vying for your trust and they're selling you on their ability to fulfill your dreams and avoid your nightmares, but it's all guesswork and speculation. Here are some facts: no one knows the future; we're in a new world; the future may not resemble the past, yet their models depend on that; and 40 percent of their financial planning strategies fail. Are you willing to risk that? What you need to do is arm yourself with some investment basics.

I come to the writing of this book as one of the longest-practicing financial advisors in the United States. I have been called the "Dean of Financial Planning." I started one of the first financial planning firms in America in 1970. I have done a call-in radio program for many years, and I see myself as the old gladiator. I've been in the arena. I've been bloodied and I've been kicked around. I've won battles and lost them. All those experiences combine to establish the viewpoints and convictions I live and practice by. It is all a part of who I am—a participant, not a theoretician. *There is an alternative to Wall Street that can save billions of investor dollars and untold thousands of retirees from devastation. It is in the insurance company system of retirement, and I want to help you to see the truth and help you to have a successful future.* That's what this book is about.

For all that happened in the earlier stages of my career, this stage is the one that feels most urgent and most important. I view myself now as a rebel against what is taking place in the financial services industry and in financial planning practices everywhere.

The industry is putting out information that is loaded with myths and deceptions, and many of the people who are doing it don't even realize it. It would be as though you're a doctor who went to a college completely funded by Eli Lilly or Pfizer, and all you learned is what they wanted you to learn. You would be isolated from the full reality of your profession. You wouldn't know what you didn't know.

My greatest teachers are the people who come into my office emotionally devastated or call in to my radio program in a similar condition. These are hard-working people who listened to the conventional wisdom. My practice requires me to critique and condemn the conventional wisdom, because it does not work. The number of people whose security has been compromised by what the securities industry has told them is vast. I never knew this until I began doing my radio program. Hundreds of people have called in, living proof of the breadth of bad advice out there. If you're just a practitioner, an individual person doing this, maybe you see 20 to 30 clients in a year. I have a much larger number of people emailing and calling me—65-year-old women, in difficult straits and plagued by anxiety. One woman, 58-years-old, never married, with no pension, was a customer of one of the biggest banks in the country. She went there because she could feel safe at this bank—that was her belief. The bank's investment officers have placed 100 percent of her assets in the stock market—50 percent in aggressive growth, 50 percent regular growth. She lost more than 80 percent of her portfolio value in the downturn of '08, and her so-called advisors have not made a change in strategy since then. All they have to say is: "Stay the course, be patient, it will come back." I see so much of this so-called guidance that I really have become a cynic.

And I have discovered since 9/11 that we—financial people and you, the investor—are in a world we've never been in, and many of the pillars of this financial planning industry don't hold in the new economy. There is no option but to rebel. This book is the gladiator who speaks the truth, and I want it to be controversial, because there needs to be an outcry and Americans need to know the financial reality that surrounds them.

My mission is to design retirement plans that are as foolproof as possible. My job: Focus on the negative things that can destroy the plan, because bad things happen. Retirement management is not about wishful thinking; it's about confronting reality and making sure that a stable and predictable lifelong income is provided under any economic circumstances.

Part of that mission is to inform seniors that many of the so-called pillars of traditional financial planning are false and dangerous to their financial health. Wall Street's plans have failed investors and left millions of people financially shaken, insecure and distrustful. I can present alternative plans developed to protect investors' money against market losses. Be advised: *You do not have to risk your assets in order to have the opportunity to grow your wealth.*

The problem about living on one's income has been solved. Income for life for both husband and wife is a reality. Here's another part of my mission: Delivering the message that there's hope. You have the opportunity to grow your assets without being exposed to market risk. It is not too good to be true, and it is not too late to begin.

I am not a prophet of doom. I am not a pessimist. I am a realist. Yet my realism is forcing me to be pessimistic. It's long been true that forewarned is forearmed, and that is my intent. This book has been written for people who are approaching or are in retirement.

I reflect very often on guidance found in Proverbs 21:5: *Plans of the diligent lead to profits as surely as haste leads to poverty.* That sums up my approach to financial planning.

CHAPTER 2

RETIREMENT CRISIS IN AMERICA

One of the problems for retirees of the present era is the disappearance of the defined-benefit pension plan. Beyond that trend, of pension plans not being provided by employers, is the prospect of the pension plan that is in existence but it has the threat of being taken away should the company fail to fund it appropriately. Pensions have become less dependable. The 401(k) has become less dependable because of the shock of the downturn of '08, when the average 401(k) fell 28 percent.

According to the Investment Company Institute, of the 90 percent of private sector workers who had access to a pension plan in 1975—people who were covered by a traditional, defined-benefit pension—only 20 percent of them ever received any income from those plans.

Looking back, 401(k)s were created in 1978, offering the ostensibly valuable benefit of allowing a worker who moved from job to job to be able to take that savings plan with him. Prior to that, there had been no portability of retirement savings accounts or plans. But the challenge that came upon the 401(k) worker as demonstrated in 2008, and why it's less dependable, is that they saw themselves as completely at the mercy of the markets. Most people today would say the 401(k) experiment has been a failure.

We have entered into what might be called the Era of Unretirement. These less-than-dependable 401(k) arrangements, plus the sharp drop in home values, jolted Americans who had been going along with a decent amount of confidence in their finances. People got the sense in 2008, with stock market and real estate market downturns, that in reality they possessed scant control over their finances and their prospects. The result was a seismic shift in their psychological view of retirement, because market volatility had stung them, and, going forward, it would be a persistent concern. To add to their concerns, somewhat paradoxically, were the statistics showing that people in general were living longer. All these factors put together have produced what we call America's Retirement Crisis. That's the state of things—we are in a crisis. Now, if you do know and recognize, as I do, that there are countermeasures, you might join me in rephrasing that to the Retirement Challenge.

Here are three major problems for the older member of the workforce to acknowledge:
- Increased market volatility.
- Increasing cost of living.
- Increased life expectancies.

That is the triple play—or if you take the most dire view, that's the tsunami—that lies ahead. Longevity is an oddly unnerving proposition. You will often hear people in their 60s say, offhandedly, "I don't want to live to be 93 like my Aunt Mable," and then go about their business. If they are paying attention to news from the scientific community, they will understand that stem cell research is advancing. We may very well solve some of these chronic illnesses that are so debilitating to seniors, especially Alzheimer's. As a financial person, my job is to make certain you have an income for life, however long that is.

Let's take a moment and look ahead. As you view the world and ponder reasonable planning strategies, do you see things getting simpler or more complex? Do you see things getting safer or more dangerous? Are you expecting conditions to become more stable or more volatile? In each case, it must be the latter. And then you put those questions with that perfect storm and there is a great anxiety in America's retirement worker. The confidence level of Americans is at an all-time low.

Americans for a Secure Retirement retained Ernst & Young to analyze the likelihood that middle income Americans would outlive their financial assets. Current data and a comprehensive set of forecasting tools produced an unhappy answer. It said that three out of five middle-class new retirees could expect to outlive their money as they attempt to maintain their pre-retirement standard of living. Three out of five, and why? According to the Ernst & Young report retirees will have to reduce their standard of living primarily because of fluctuating investment returns and, factored in with that, the probability of spending more years in retirement. Again, it's that perfect storm.

And that's why you, as the investor, and I, as the advisor, are going to develop a solution. We have a way to take the risk out of the market. It's a compelling and proven investment tool that the brokers and the myth makers don't want people to know about. We live, as some realize, in what has become a pension-less society. People now must depend on themselves. The pension-less society was the term plainly used in the Ernst & Young report, discussing the difficulties that lie ahead for so many Americans. It is so important that they get a handle on their assets today and protect those hard-earned, hard-saved assets from fluctuating market returns.

The majority of Americans work for small-business owners like me, who typically do not provide pensions for their employees. The old-time, defined-benefit pension was a short-lived perquisite in our economic structure. What you have as you head toward the end of your earning years is what you've worked to build in those "pension-like" vehicles, your 401(k)s. But here's another statistic, which came out of a survey by one of the major players in the retirement annuity market: More than 80 percent of U.S. workers have stated that they were going to need at least three years to rebuild their savings as a result of the financial collapse of 2008 and the Great Recession that has ensued. That's how far they had fallen. Even given the statistic, you wonder if the three-year estimate was realistic. Then the question becomes: In the volatile equities markets we've been through since 2008, how much rebuilding really happened?

According to the firm of Towers Watson, four in 10 workers are planning to delay their retirement so that they can accumulate more money to try to live well. "Whether by necessity or choice, many Baby Boomers expect to work until their 65th birthday or later," the report said. It further noted: "The percentage of workers who expect to retire after 65 has increased steadily over the last 20 years from 11 percent in 1991, to 20 percent in 2000, and up to 33 percent in 2010." One-third of the workforce speaks of looking to extend their working years to try to make up for the losses. Meanwhile, what's to say that once they retire we don't get whacked in 2013 or shortly thereafter with another market free-fall? Things are more uncertain today than people even realize.

Americans see themselves as powerless—at the mercy of the markets and at the mercy of inflation. Nor do they have confidence in what their brokers are telling them. The brokers are giving them the company line: "Invest in the market so you can offset inflation." For that advice to work, these beloved markets would need to turn out consistent gains. Meanwhile, the opposite is plenty likely. The stock and mutual fund markets have been the source of depleted portfolios. But the mantra never shifts. "Invest in the market, hang in there, it's going to come back," is the message people hear.

Russ's Rules for Retirees

1. Beware of false prophets. Some people have their interest ahead of yours.

2. Utilize big mistake/little mistake mentality. A big mistake could be the loss of 20 percent or more of your portfolio. A little mistake could be a lower return than the market's. If you cannot afford to make a big mistake, do not expose your assets to such a decision, and accept little mistakes.

---

3. Get it in writing. Make sure your financial planner has understood your goals and gives them back to you in written form for your approval.

4. Seniors, err on the side of safety. Remember, markets were not created to have a goal that matches yours.

5. There are two kinds of money: Golden goose money, the foundation of your plan, which is used to guarantee essential income now or in the future; and turkey money, that which can be gobbled up through spending or market loss. Protect the golden goose, and once you've done that, spend and enjoy the speculative money.

6. Make certain essential income needs are funded with safe, guaranteed investments. For retirees taking income from their portfolios, know that asset allocation and diversification do little to prevent loss and/or extend the life of your retirement account.

7. Understand negative sequence of returns. In a distribution portfolio, the loss of even 10 percent during the first three to four years of retirement could shorten the life of your fund by 10 to 15 years.

8. Do not expose your retirement portfolio to possibility of loss.

9. Do not place a variable annuity in your IRA.

10. Establish an emergency fund that will allow you to plan for the unexpected. You'll also have a fund to tap during market downs.

11. Do not have more than 25 percent of your retirement portfolio in equities.

Source: Putnam Investments, June 2011.

CHAPTER 3

DEBUNKING WALL STREET'S MYTHS OF FINANCIAL PLANNING

I t is important for the reader to understand a couple of basics, one of them being, "What is the definition of market risk?" It starts with the plain fact that the stock market can move in two directions, and when it moves in a negative direction it lowers the value of your equity holdings—that's market risk. The other kind of risk is called interest rate risk, and most people are not familiar with this. It deals with bonds, which most people perceive to be their safe assets, and when interest rates move up, the value of a bond moves down.

Yes, there can be loss in something as safe as a government bond, because of rising interest rates. Let's look at 20-year U.S. Treasury bonds, offered at a rate of, for example, 3 percent. If at some time over the 20-year period interest rates move up and the 3 percent rate becomes very unattractive and you wanted to sell your guaranteed government bond, the government's not going to buy it back for its full value until the end of 20 years. Anyone else who would buy it will do so at what's called a discount, and you would therefore lose money. And the mathematics on that is that for every 1 percent interest rate increase, the value of that 20-year bond will fall approximately 10 percent.

Therefore, I encourage people to beware—be *aware*—of interest rate risk and *beware* of purchasing long-term investments that are regarded as safe because of the risk of selling them before their maturity and incurring a dramatic loss of principal.

I encourage investors not to seek a higher return by purchasing a longer-term maturity bond because of interest rate risk. I would also advise them not to turn to debt instruments in a low-interest-rate environment because of the risk associated with any long-term commitment to bonds that you purchase. They likely would be sold at a discount if you needed to liquidate the holding, given that interest rates are likely to move up during your holding period. One of my concerns is that the average financial planner still continues to blend portfolios for retirees using the ratio of approximately 60 percent equities and 40 percent bonds. Historically they have made that purchase of bonds to manage or diminish volatility. But now, if the stock market moves down and interest rates move up, we will be looking at the entire portfolio losing money.

The highest interest rates that any readers of this book would be able to remember will be those during the Jimmy Carter administration. That's when you could purchase CDs paying the now-unthinkable rate of 18 percent to 20 percent. Much has changed since the mid-1980s, in the debt market as well as elsewhere.

So somebody who today is a 50-year-old financial advisor was 24 years old when those sky-high CD rates were available. Over this advisor's entire professional life, he has only known interest rates to move down and bond prices to rise. But now we're entering a period in which interest rates could be going up for the next 20 or 30 years, and most advisors have no idea how to manage a portfolio in a rising interest rate climate. Bonds are often associated with safety, and seldom discussed as being what they are—an investment that can move both down and up in value. Today's typical financial advisor has never practiced in this era of uncertainty and low interest rates and is not equipped to manage money in it.

Let's look at a couple in their 50s named Tom and Angela, whom we will get to know better in the next chapter. Tom couldn't stop wondering why, after carefully following his broker's advice, he and Angela had incurred such significant losses in the downturns of 2000 to 2002 and then again in 2008. They even lost in their bonds, which are supposed to be safe. They found themselves muttering the same observation repeatedly: "We did everything we were told, yet we lost a major part of our nest egg."

Tom, as an engineer, felt compelled to question the foundational theories of financial planning. He thought back to his college years and a professor who would so often turn to the class and ask: "Does the evidence support the hypothesis?" Tom realized that the language and references used by his financial advisor were quite peppered with phrases suggesting scientific measurement and technically advanced forecasting tools. The impression was that this all amounted to a legitimate science. For example, the advisor used what are called Monte Carlo simulations, which, they say, provide a 95 percent level of confidence in the tested outcome. Any branch or field of study can employ the Monte Carlo test protocol. They are based on computational algorithms that use repeated random sampling to compute results.

In the case of Tom's broker, the sophisticated-sounding application of the Monte Carlo simulation made future performance seem reliable, because so many factors had been accounted for. The broker told our investing couple that their government bonds were guaranteed—fine, that's true if the eventuality is that Tom and Angela would hold them to maturity. The broker also told Tom and Angela that the variable annuity he was selling them was safely insulated from stock market losses. Furthermore, by using asset allocation they would be "shielded from downturns." He further told them: "We've selected some of the finest mutual funds, and as a trained professional advisor, I'm able to guide you through that selection process."

All these statements of confidence came and went, offering temporary reassurance. Meanwhile, Tom and Angela would end up experiencing two major downturns, and in both, suffered major losses. Tom's conclusion was the hypothesis used in financial planning is hogwash. Success is based on luck. Remember, this is Tom's conclusion. Success is based on luck. I'm lucky when the market goes up, and I'm a victim of it when it goes down, no matter what they tell me and no matter what the most sophisticated computer models have told us to do. It seems to be the luck factor that plays the largest role in my success or failure. Financial planning is not a science.

The scientists who developed Monte Carlo simulations came up with an excellent tool for calculating outcomes, but one wonders what they would think about applying that tool to personal finance. Likely they would have suspected it as window dressing or a smoke-screen—which it assuredly is. In financial planning, it has represented the use of averages—average rate of return, average rate of inflation, and then projected withdrawal rates from this or that investment. The financial planning industry knows that over the past 100 years, the stock market has averaged an 8.8 percent return.

Why is it, then, that if in fact we simulated a retirement with an 8.8 percent average return, a 6 percent withdrawal rate, and a 3 percent inflation rate, that the portfolio runs out of money 45 percent of the time? It is because averages do not work. Markets do not move in averages. An average return of 8.8 percent is literally never achieved in the market. There might be a 12 percent return or a 4 percent loss, but the most important aspect in retirement planning during the distribution phase of retirement is the prevention of loss—and the sequence of returns.

At any point when the market experiences a couple of years of downward movement, there is virtually zero chance of that portfolio being able to support the withdrawals. And the fallacy of using averages is that markets do not move in average. The Monte Carlo device uses multiple simulations and multiple assumptions of what a market can do, therefore it may indeed produce results that are theoretically interesting. But it is still not based upon actual market returns, and while it brings much more information into the decision-making process, it is shown that it does not produce any more accuracy. Plus, this is an individual's money we are talking about —when the pseudo-scientific calculations don't work, it's not just numbers on a computer screen. So, the caution here is that while

Monte Carlo presents itself as very scientific and reliable, history has not shown that to be true.

It's appropriate at this time to look at a statement from a highly recommended book on the subject. The title of the book is *Unveiling the Retirement Myth* and the author is Jim C. Otar. In the book, Otar writes:

> *We have fooled our clients far too long with models using steady growth rates. Now we're again trying to fool them, this time with randomness called Monte Carlo simulations. The greatest danger and impediment to the advancement of mathematics of distribution is the fabrication of useless studies by researchers using Monte Carlo. I cringe every time I look at a publication that includes the words, 'using a Monte Carlo simulator,' 'scientific study,' 'our conclusion is,' in the same article. Our money, trillions of dollars, is managed based on such flawed models and assumptions.*

The next fallacy to be confronted is found in that statement by Tom's advisor when he said: "Your government bonds will be guaranteed." And herein we talk about while government bonds are guaranteed by the United States—by the government issuing them—the guarantee is for the interest payments to be made and for the full amount of the purchase of that bond to be redeemed at the maturity date. If in fact that bond is liquidated prior to that, a reduced or greater value will be received. A reduced value, of course, is based upon interest rates rising. Interest rates did jump up in 2008, and the value of many bonds plummeted as much as 30 percent. And 2008 showed many people, that what they thought had complete safety was subject to the fluctuations of interest, and people must be aware of this. It is one of the greatest risks today for the investing public, to become aware that what they think to be safe is subject to principal diminishment as interest rates rise. We call it "interest rate risk," and as I will explain further in the chapter entitled "Investment Basics."

The myths that substituted for actual prudence in Tom and Angela's case also included this one: "Your variable annuity has a 5 percent guarantee." Variable annuities, just to be clear, are some of the most expensive investments an individual can purchase, and I personally am not a fan of them. Variable annuities often come with guarantees, but they are for the most part grossly misunderstood. The guarantee is not on the principal but on a separate account called an "income account." It has nothing to do with the principal amount of the asset. More will be discussed on this in a later chapter.

If the reader can bear it, I will add yet another delusion perpetrated by the industry: "You are broadly diversified, and therefore you are well-insulated from stock market losses." Diversification, as a brokerage advisor defines it, means owning many of the same type of asset. For example, in the case of stock market investing, you would own many stocks. For the mutual fund investor who is "diversified," it means owning an array of mutual funds. Yes, there is an enduring adage about not putting all your eggs in one basket, and it endures for a reason. But it should not be applied to the situations I've just described. Yes, theoretically I agree with diversification; however, it has been shown that diversification between large-company stock, medium-company stock and small-company stocks, as well as international stocks, has almost no bearing on the safety or the growth of a portfolio over time.

Again I will rely on Jim C. Otar, whose comments on diversification I'll paraphrase. He writes that diversification has virtually no impact on an investor's attempt to avoid losses or increase returns over any given period of time. The reality is, when markets decline and bad things happen, all stocks go down. No amount of diversification prevents that. That will come as a shock to most people.

Another myth concerns asset allocation, which is at least a sacred cow and more likely the Holy Grail of conventional financial advisors. By definition, asset allocation is the blending of two or more different asset classes. An asset class would be, for example, equities, cash, bonds, gold, natural resources, real estate; and most financial advisors only allocate assets between equities, bonds and cash. Asset allocation is also a useful tool during the accumulation years of a portfolio. But, in a distribution portfolio, asset allocation has been shown to have little or no effect on the length of time that the portfolio will survive.

Whether assets are allocated to 100 percent equities, 60 percent equities or 20 percent equities, it will have little to no effect on how long that portfolio will survive, because there is a major difference between accumulation planning and distribution planning. The most important aspect of distribution planning is insulating a portfolio from any loss, and asset allocation does not do that. At any period of time—and this goes back to 1900—the probability of a portfolio losing one-tenth of its value in the stock market is more than 20 percent. In other words, you have a 20 percent chance in any year of losing more than 10 percent of your holdings. If that happens to you in a distribution portfolio, the chances of the portfolio being depleted during your lifetime increase dramatically. And if that loss is significantly higher than 10 percent in a year, it's nearly impossible to recover it, no matter how long you live.

Here's another vital point regarding the difference between accumulation investing and distribution investing: A market may recover, but that doesn't mean the portfolio will, because there are cash demands on that portfolio that are happening real-time. When you make a withdrawal, that's a permanent loss.

All of this hard reality of what happens to retirement portfolio using the Wall Street mindset led the accounting giant Ernst & Young to state that it expects four out of five Americans—families— to outlive their retirement assets because of increased living expenses and portfolio fluctuations—in other words, losses. But the financial planning industry is not being up front with people about the risks of their advice not working, and the result is that people fall into a false sense of security.

As you recall, Tom was assured by his broker with the statement: "We have selected some of the finest mutual funds for you." Well, again, that's a myth. There is no way to pick a mutual fund or a stock, because past performance has zero correlation to any possible future result. You can look backward with flawless descriptions or ratings of a particular mutual fund. Once the record is written, you can always sift through the results, rank the performance of all funds, and say what you will about 10 years of success. But to do that is erroneous. In my opinion it's a practice that should not even be permitted, because there is no correlation between past and future, not even when you're looking at the recent past. Maybe especially in that scenario.

We can easily pull out the record showing the top 30 mutual funds according to return on investment in the period between 1990 and 1999. When we survey that grouping, we see that these top performers turned in the impressive average annual rate of return of 27 percent.

Then, for the next decade, those same funds averaged a 4 percent loss.

As a matter of fact, something that's not written there is that of those top 30 funds, not one of them, as you survey the ensuing decade, managed to land in the top 1000 in terms of rating. That's how far they fell. And that's the key point there

Before I started doing an extensive amount of work with hybrid annuities, I would see my clients' accounts fall in difficult times, then I would think, "What mutual fund could I move them to, in order to turn this trend around?" I studied the possibilities tirelessly to answer that question. Looking back on that futility, I now ask myself what it would be like if myths were tossed out and real honesty were employed. You would have couples like Tom and Angela sitting in the offices of their brokers hearing this statement: "We actually have no way of selecting a mutual fund that gives us any idea of how well they're going to do." That's what honesty would look like and sound like.

This business is guesswork, if you go about it according to Wall Street's conventional thinking. And of all mythical statements the real lie is: "I'm going to manage your money." That's the pledge of commitment you will hear as you're making the commitment in the broker's office. You are sitting in front of him, thinking about Monte Carlo simulations, feeling confident, and he seals the deal. He's got a nice mahogany desk and a suit and a tie on, and he looks you directly in the eye and says, "Glad you're here. We're going to manage your money." And you feel good, and you leave, and as the front door hits you in the backside on your way out, he's picking up the telephone making his next prospect call. That's his business model – work hard prospecting, troll for new business, line up appointments, and get people to sign on the dotted line.

So-called financial advisors at mahogany desks for the most part do not manage portfolios. They build you the little pie chart, and then once you're gone that pie chart might as well be cast in concrete. Things drift along, until one day—it could be during a downturn or an upturn—the phone rings and it's Tom saying, "What the heck is going on? This portfolio of mine is down dramatically." Or else he's up very modestly while a true bull market is stampeding along. Then he says, "What's the deal? I'm barely up for the year and every day they're saying the markets are setting records for gains." The answer is generally calm and measured. It goes something like, "I was just thinking about you, Tom, and I happen to have your file right out here on my desk. Why don't you come on in?" And you come in, and he says, "You know, I think you're right. But we can do better, so we probably should make a change." And in Missouri, they call that closing the barn door after the horse is halfway down the road.

Well, financial planners have no skin in the game, and that upsets people. And I would like to see some things changed: I'd like to see that financial planners who are charging fees don't get a fee if the market goes down or if the client loses money. But their answer to that is that it's not permitted by law. Well, the law is made by the financial planning industry itself, the Securities and Exchange Commission, which for the most part is controlled by Wall Street. Do you think they couldn't change that?

The fact is, they're told they're not going to change that, because it would take billions of revenue out of their pockets. I mean, the law's not made by Moses; it's made by the people who run the system. I am talking about the SEC, the people who looked the other way when whistle-blowers were making noises to them about Bernie Madoff. They went through the motions on one of the biggest scams in human history. The SEC made a dozen preliminary investigations or at least inquiries and didn't turn in Bernie. He was allowed to continue bilking people.

There's not one 401(k) plan in the country that has been allowed to have a fixed annuity, which is a guaranteed place to put your money, or a savings account, because Wall Street doesn't sell these products and Wall Street writes the rules. They're the largest contributors to the legislators who sit in Washington and draft the rules, and Wall Street knows very well that if there were a fixed annuity choice for investors to turn to the world would be vastly different. I ask myself where all these troubled people would be if their assets had been in hybrid fixed annuities instead of in their tanking mutual funds. It would be a much happier scenario, and that's an understatement.

People, if they had known about this option, would have flocked to it. Wall Street companies' fees would have taken a body blow. We are talking about the loss of billions and billions. This is about the money and Wall Street controlling America's retirement.

Let me give you the final bullet here from Tom and Angela. The one prior was, "We selected some of the finest mutual funds." The next one was their advisor telling them, "As a trained financial professional, I am able to guide you through retirement." But the fact is, from an educational standpoint, the financial planning industry has virtually no investment training for the distribution phase of retirement.

Remember, there are two phases of financial planning: There is the accumulation phase, and then there is the distribution phase. The accumulation phase is when you're in your working years, and if you have a loss—here's a key difference—you have ongoing contributions to help cover that. Likewise, during that accumulation phase, the single most important attribute of your plan is, indeed, asset allocation. However, it can't be one-time asset allocation, as in make the pie chart, get the signature, and forget about it.

Once you are in the distribution phase, no further contributions are coming in. At that point, asset allocation plays no role in extending the life of a distribution portfolio. The most important aspect of a distribution portfolio is sequence of returns. How do you manage the sequence of returns? And the key is, we know that if there is a loss within the first four years, even if it is only 10 percent, the likelihood of that distribution portfolio being able to last your lifetime is greatly diminished.

So the question becomes, how do you manage properly the distribution portfolio? And the financial planning industry has not trained its people. And I would venture to say that most financial planners have no idea what I just said, that they don't know that there is a difference between managing a distribution portfolio and an accumulation portfolio. As your retirement years commence, you find yourself starting the distribution phase and the reality is this: If bad things happen and markets go down, your financial advisor is not an integral part of the decision-making process. It's really the luck factor. And the difference between a successful and an unsuccessful retirement is—watch this now, nobody's ever said this before —*managing the luck factor*. How do you set up your assets to avoid bad luck? "Bad luck" meaning the market drops.

The remedy is not what you do with your *portfolio* but what you do with your *assets*.

CHAPTER 4

INVESTMENT BASICS FOR RETIREMENT PLANNING

Retirement planning is a process of designing and following a strategy that will provide a lifelong income for the retiree and his or her spouse. Just to repeat, I am talking about a solid, viable strategy, not a grab bag of wishful thinking and tired truisms. The reliable, real-world retirement plan cannot be and is not based on historic average rates of return and average rates of inflation, as are so many Wall Street forecasts.

Let's use a case study: Tom and his wife, Angela, whom we met in the previous chapter, are like many Americans planning for retirement. We meet them in 2011, when they are in their early 50s, their children are raised, and they've got to start seriously thinking about their future. They need to look ahead to the point when they leave the workforce and are no longer in the accumulation phase of their lives. Planning is imperative at this point, and Tom is indeed ready, but Angela has a nagging feeling that all may not be as certain as Tom had painted.

Tom also has underlying concerns. Can he really depend on his full pension for life? Living expenses have been rising. Had he saved enough? Would the markets continue to be volatile? Tom sat one day and reflected on the unprecedented times he and Angela had experienced over the past decade. In 2008, they lost nearly 50 percent of their nest egg. Their home value was sliced in half. The rules of investing their broker preached for so long had failed. Banks had mismanaged themselves and Wall Street's greed and mismanagement seemingly removed any and all of its credibility as a source of information and guidance. This gave Tom great concern. Whom or what could he trust for his and Angela's future security?

Tom walked home from the corner store one afternoon through the sunshine. He was smiling on the outside but had a knot in his stomach. Would his savings be enough for the two of them to supplement their pension and inflation-proof their future? He had another concern, one he had not shared with his wife. What if he were to get sick and need long-term care? A scenario like that could wipe out the 401(k). "If I passed away," thought Tom, "Angela would get a reduced pension and only one of our Social Security checks. That's not much security—a reduced pension, one Social Security check and a diminished 401(k). How would Angela live? What would inflation to do her future and standard of living?"

Tom thinks back over the last decade. They lost a lot in the downturn of 2001–02, and they made it up, only to lose it again in 2008. An entire decade of not a penny gained. As a matter of fact, they're still down in August of 2011, versus where they were in early 2008. What lay ahead? What would the stock market hold in the future as they tried to grow and preserve their nest egg?

The next day Tom finds that his anxiety is still with him and he begins to reflect on how he has endeavored to plan and prepare for this stage of his and Angela's life—what he had hoped would be a peaceful and enjoyable time. He had an advisor, yet even with his advice, Tom's investment rose and fell with the ups and downs of the market. He found himself wondering what real value his broker's advice brought. He had put aside the exact amount his broker's financial plan called for, based on the stock market's 100–year average growth rate of 8.8 percent, at 3 percent inflation. Tom was shown that he had plenty of money to retire on.

Now he was told, "Roll your 401(k) money into an IRA of stocks and bond mutual funds and put a big chunk into a variable annuity with a 5 percent guaranteed account, and sit back, stay the course, don't get out—can't do that, or you'll miss the next upturn —and don't worry, because it will all come back." That's the typical investment advice that people get.

Most people do not know why they are investing. Every time I give a presentation or speak in front of a group, I ask the audience, "Why is it that you invest?" And people sit dumbfounded. Gradually they begin to offer answers. "So I can grow my money." "I invest so that I can grow but only with moderate risk." The answers are all investment-related. And the answer is this: You are investing your money so that at a point in the future you can turn it into a pension plan. You invest so that you can create a future income.

The idea is to develop an income for life. You are investing toward that one goal. Some people will immediately need to stream that income, if they don't have a pension. Others will need it perhaps 10 years after they retire, specifically to inflation-proof their pensions, which are not normally tied to cost of living, unless we're talking about government employees, bless their hearts.

The most important aspect of a successful investment retirement plan is having enough money to guarantee that your "essential income" (the money to cover your fixed expenses) will be there for you and your spouse for your lifetime, and that it has the opportunity to increase with inflation. The greatest risk to one's retirement is a loss within the first two years in which distributions are being taken. So, the primary reason to invest is to create that income for life.

You know why Wall Street doesn't talk about that? Because it doesn't have products that will make that happen. You can't do it with stocks. You can't do it with dividends. You can't do it with bond interest. Those are the three ways Wall Street has you prepare to retire, and they are insufficient or worse.

Another investment basic I share with people in my presentations is this: The rate of saving is more important than the rate of return. Most of the money that is put aside for your eventual use will be there because of disciplined saving, and that is more important than rate of return. We have essential expenses and discretionary expenses. As a financial planner I can assure clients that their essential expenses will be covered for their lifetime and their spouse's lifetime, regardless of the economy. Having assured that, we can proceed in our planning from essential money to discretionary money. Those funds we could look at putting into the stock market if the client wishes. But I don't want economic, political or military risk threatening an asset that is intended to fund an essential expense. Wall Street doesn't preach this. That precaution isn't part of its thinking.

As we build this style of plan, following the stated goal of income for life, we are highly conscious of guarding the client against outliving his or her assets. My clients are familiar with an acronym I have developed, SIPS. It stands for Structured Income Portfolio Strategy. And it's based upon the premise—and this is an investment basic—that no asset will be placed into a security, a stock, if it is needed for support within 12 to 15 years. Therefore, our Structured Income Portfolio System calls for setting up buckets of money. Bucket number one would pay an income for, in many cases, five years. Bucket number two accumulates for five years and then pays an income out in years six through 10. Bucket number three accumulates for 10 years and pays out all of its money as needed.

We get to bucket number four, and that is the portion of the assets I will expose to the upside and downside potential of the stock market. This can be done thanks to what we've established using the first three of the buckets. With the fourth bucket, our vital element is time. We have the benefit of time on our side to absorb the ups and downs. So, unlike the Wall Street system of retirement that immediately puts people into the stock market in hopes that their holdings go up, we delay the need to access any of our stock market funds for 15 years. This is my strategy to combine the certainty of what are called fixed hybrid annuities for the first 15 years, and then market assets beyond. So it is a disciplined structure for safety with assurance and then opportunity. But take note, I am talking about opportunity that's deferred—to absorb the volatility of the market and provide the best opportunity for success.

Now, the only way for an individual to have income that he or she cannot outlive is to purchase an annuity from the insurance industry. An annuity is the only vehicle that can offer a lifetime of income. Rather than taking the gamble of running out of money, we effectively shift the risk to the insurance company. And that is the one way of guaranteeing that you cannot outlive your funds. The insurance company, which knows risk better than anyone and is compelled by law to minimize it at every turn, will pay the annual sum it is obligated to pay if you live to be the age of Methuselah. When we get to Chapter 7, you will learn in great detail about the value and importance of annuities.

As you have likely noticed, the topic of risk is what we've really been addressing all along. If I am to cover the basics of investing I surely need to give the reader an understanding of it, as it effects retirement planning.

To begin with, there's market risk and there's interest rate risk. Market risk is the stock market, the equities market, moving up and down. Interest rate risk is the impact of rising interest rates on investments such as bonds. As interest goes up, the value of a bond goes down. Bonds, when you purchase them, have maturity dates. But there is a resale market for bonds—that's what the nightly newscaster is referring to when he says, "The bond market was down today," or that it was up. Bonds that already exist have set and unchanging yields. The day after an investor buys them, the environment is a little different, and that environment continues to evolve, economically and politically. So the institution that sold the investor that bond may have to offer a higher interest rate to sell bonds to someone else a few months later. The investor who bought that first bond doesn't have to keep it to maturity; he can sell it on the resale market. But it won't be so attractive now, because newly issued bonds are paying a higher rate. Obviously that also happens in reverse. So bond prices move in the opposite direction of interest rates. It's called interest rate risk. I want people to understand that, because interest rates today are terribly low, thus there is great risk in owning such things as government bonds, municipal bonds, and high-rate corporate bonds. If interest rates go up, the value of those assets will fall.

I will have clients identify and tally up their essential expenses. I will also have them determine when they will need to turn on the income spigot of their plan. Some people will be quite slow to turn it on, even when the time arrives when that segment of their funds in the plan was supposed to be accessible. They might have their pension and don't need to turn on their income spigot until inflation has kicked in. People either need money immediately or they need it later, but at some point most people do need it.

Education and persistence, as well as getting professional advice—those are basics. Be committed to finding alternatives to Wall Street's traditional thinking. As you proceed, be committed to learning, and be persistent, don't get discouraged.

You must also understand the difference between accumulation planning and distribution planning. Most, or virtually all, financial advisors have been trained only in accumulation planning. And the techniques for accumulation planning are not the same as the techniques for distribution or income planning. That's why a crucial investment basic is this: Find yourself an income or distribution-planning specialist. The investment industry has virtually no training for distribution planning. Your advisor may state that he specializes in both, but he more than likely is not trained to do so. The advisor who got you to the pre-retirement stage may not be the one to go forward with. Again, we will address that point in greater detail in Chapter 8.

Finally, here is one more investment basic for you to think about: *The shoestring's tied to money.* In my hometown of Hillsdale, Michigan, there was an IGA grocery store. I went there often as a little boy and remember the place well. Each time I walked in, the first thing that caught my attention was the sign above the front door: "Low prices, high quality, great service." And then in little words below that it said, "Pick any two." The world of investing is like that. There are shoestrings tied to money. The three aspects of any investment are liquidity, growth and safety. And just like the IGA grocery store sign so plainly advised, you can pick any two. You really can't have all three. You can have liquidity and growth, but you'd give up safety. You can have safety and liquidity, but you'd give up growth. Understand that in all of life we have trade-offs, and it is true as well in the world of money.

This brings us to the crux of the Jalbert philosophy of money management, best expressed in question form: *If I want to grow my money, would I give up liquidity or would I give up safety?* The right answer for my clients is to give up liquidity. If I, as a retiree or pre-retiree, could increase my rate of return simply by giving up some liquidity, I would trade that any day. My choice would not be to give up safety.

CHAPTER 5

MYTHS AND DECEITS OF MUTUAL FUNDS

I cofounded Oakland Financial Group, one of our country's first fee-oriented financial planning firms in 1970. I have been part of this industry since its early days, and I, too, bought into the many myths I have been discussing with you. So let's look at the path of my own realizations, which I drew from a set of critical questions about mutual funds. Were they just put together as a sales gimmick that sounded logical or was there something behind them? Take a look at the following graph showing mutual fund performance from 1960 to 1979. In that period, you see a market that goes up and down; it actually ends up going sideways, but there's a big dip, and then it comes back and goes down. Now look down at the next graph, which is even more dramatic. It looks like stairs going up to the skies. That's 1980–1999. For the stock market, that period was stunningly and unusually positive. Finally look at the period from 2000 forward. That one shows big ups and dramatic downs. So, that graph in the middle, 1980–99, becomes a relative oddity. It's a segment of financial history that people have become fixated on. It's the period that, to this day, gives the industry license to say: "Hey, don't get out now, because you'll miss the next upturn."

DOW JONES INDUSTRIAL AVERAGE (1960-1979)

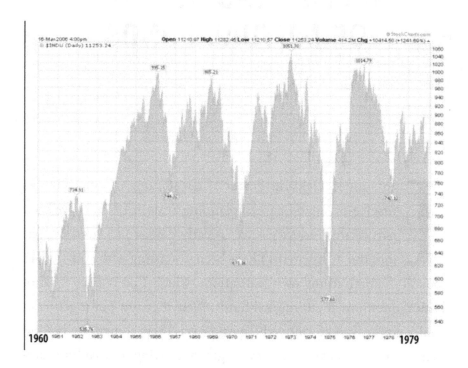

DOW JONES INDUSTRIAL AVERAGE (1980-1999)

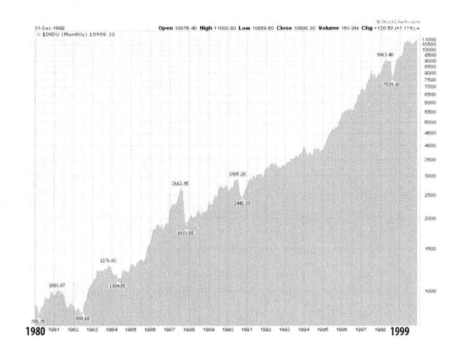

DOW JONES INDUSTRIAL AVERAGE (2000 - PRESENT)

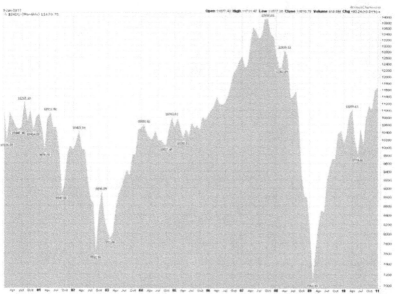

2000 to Present

These graphs show us that the world that the financial planning industry got its legs from doesn't exist anymore. It's my contention that the 20-year period in which baby boomers were funding their 401(k)s—those same people who are now in the retirement phase of their life—was an anomaly. It is a grave mistake for people to treat the 1989-99 period as something normal. That degree of positive performance never occurred at any other time in the 200-year history of the stock market. It was the largest sustained upward move ever to occur in Western civilization. It is by no means the world that we're in today, and we cannot take the theories of an aberration and place them into the uncertain world of today with any degree of confidence that they'll help us.

The phrase that applies is "negative sequence of returns." If you start out your retirement with the market going up, you'll have a far different result than if you start out as the market is primarily going down. A recent Metropolitan Life study concluded that it all comes down to your portfolio's performance in the first few years of retirement. If you experience a bear market such as occurred in 2000, you might find yourself 10–15 years short of adequate retirement income. The Met Life study puts it plainly; These poor returns in the first years of retirement *cannot be mitigated using any conventional investments for asset-allocation strategy.* In other words, we in the financial business have nothing in our Wall Street system of retirement-oriented investing to defend against a negative sequence of returns.

Therefore, you need the only thing that works, the new hybrid annuity that is immune from a negative sequence of returns. It was designed for that purpose, to provide investor protection before or during the retirement years, and Wall Street doesn't have it.

What you get from your brokerage advisor is the continued—though highly questionable—confidence in mutual fund investing. The modern mutual fund industry was born about a century ago, in Boston. There were 10 mutual funds by the end of the 1920s, but they really didn't do much. Through the Depression, through World War II, there were a lot of things on the minds of people other than investing money. But the mutual fund industry continued plugging along, then experienced great expansion after World War II. By the end of 1969, those 20 funds had grown to 200. By September of 2011 that number had grown wildly, up to more than 10,000. Yes, it had good years and even good decades—but not lately, by any stretch. The average annual return for the decade ended December 31, 2010, was less than 1 percent. That's why they call it the lost decade.

That was the wake-up call to the retiree and the pre-retiree. What confronted them at the end of the first decade of this century was unpleasant, to put it mildly. Not only did people lose money in mutual funds, but also they lost greatly in terms of net worth through the big drop in home values. Our homes became worth about half what they were previously. And that began, I believe, the emotional upheaval of a lot of Americans regarding their personal wealth. They recognized that they were anything but in control of it. People had been doing so many things "right," and the outcome was poor. That's why Wall Street today doesn't have much credibility.

It was even feverishly promoting a miserable investment called collateralized mortgage obligations. And while it was pushing them, the senior executives were buying the type of options called "puts," or "put options," which means betting against the investment.

Beyond this bad behavior by the brokerages, you had a naiveté on the part of the retail-level advisors, as well as an abdication of duty on the part of the ratings agencies—Standard & Poor's, Moody's, and the others. So how the public could possibly have confidence in financial information from Wall Street is beyond most of us to see.

There has been a new round of regulation, but they are not going to cure dishonesty and greed and fight for profits. The same organizations responsible for the 2008 crisis will simply look for another avenue. And the people who can see that greed are the American investors. That's why the insurance industry, I think, will stand tall. After 150 years of integrity and safety, it is not going to buy into this stuff.

I'm not a fan of the Wall Street system of retirement. I'm not a fan of mutual funds. The industry has changed over the years. Unfortunately, it has changed more in favor of the industry than investors. The retail mutual fund industry no longer operates the way it once did. Back in the 1980s, mutual funds, I believe, had a top concern of caring for shareholders. Today, mutual funds are aimed at caring for themselves. For example, 40 years ago the average mutual fund held a stock for approximately five years. Today the average hold is less than a year.

The mutual fund industry does not practice buy and hold, yet the financial industry passes that idea on to investors. It buys and sells stocks briskly within the individual funds. This high degree of turnover, as it is known, the selling of stocks within the portfolio, creates cost and additional taxes. It has come to the point where, by investing in a mutual fund, your costs and your tax liabilities are higher than if you sat at the computer yourself and bought individual stocks. A study conducted by Ross Millie, a former pioneer professor at Boston University, states that:

> Investors may be paying up to 10 times more than they thought for their mutual fund fees. And the primary culprit is high turnover—the excessive buying and selling of securities within the portfolio in an attempt to capture short-term gains. It creates higher fees; it forces the investors to pay taxes, often even when the fund loses money, which is a double whammy. So caution; you may very well be paying fees that you are not aware of.

Another study, by the Journal of Financial Planning, found that 87 percent of all investors whose holdings are less than $1 million had their money in mutual funds. Yet it found the opposite for people who owned portfolios in excess of $1 million: 87 percent of their monies were in holdings other than mutual funds. Isn't it interesting how most top financial advisors are not big fans of mutual funds? Fees and expenses are the reason, but you're not being informed of these patterns and problems. There are games being played every day by this industry. And it's important that these games be discussed.

One of the games is to change the fund's name. Let's assume that the fund is not doing very well, so the company changes the name; research has shown that simply changing a name increases the amount of money that flows in. Several years ago, the Smith Barney Strategic Investor Fund had been losing market share. Someone noticed that the performance would have gained it the number one spot in another sector—social awareness funds. So the Smith Barney Social Awareness Fund was born, and this marketing had nothing to do with actual return on investment.

The industry has another interesting marketing ploy that makes me think of the theater business. If a play that you wanted to see came to your city, and the producers said, "This play will be closing after tomorrow's performance," there would be a rush for tickets. Mutual funds know that, and the game is called, "closing and reopening the fund." People want what they can't have, and mutual fund companies know that; so when a fund announces a closing, marketing has shown that it attracts money. So what do some companies do to build up their coffers? Well, you guessed it. They announce a closing, and then two years later, what do you think they do? They reopen it. It's called marketing; it has nothing to do with excellence. How about this: How about false performance?

Here's a related tactic they favor. They open a mutual fund and call it the XYZ Fund II; that works just as well. It, in all likelihood, does not have the same manager and it may not have the same objective as its apparent predecessor, XYZ Fund, but it succeeds in attracting a flood of money.

We've all seen the full-page ads by the big mutual fund companies in our local newspaper or financial periodical that claim Five Star, Morningstar ratings: "Three of our funds have received Morningstar's highest awards." Well, isn't that something—but there's something that we in the business call an incubator fund, and it's probably the most devious game in the mutual fund business.

Here's how it works: The company sets up a large series of funds, as many as—believe it or not—500 funds, which are called "private" funds. And maybe the company wants to manage them using some new strategies or ideas. So it lets them bump along for about three years and then evaluates the series, because the mutual fund monitoring agency, Morningstar, demands that a fund have at least three years' history before it rates it. So what if, in fact, 497 of the funds were really not much more than garbage? That's easy, the company takes the three that did well and closes the others before the word gets out, and because these three did well, the company applies to Morningstar and receives a five-star rating. These funds are called incubator funds, and the Securities and Exchange Commission allows the past performance of these relatively small private funds to be carried forward.

Now think about it: Say you and I are doing this, and maybe we've got $10 million in the funds, we run the full-page ad, and $100 million comes in. The funds become what we in the business call "bloated." It's not as easy to manage $100 million as it is $10 million, and the performance suffers. But that's OK because it's marketing, and it has nothing to do with excellence, and all companies do this.

How about that: False reporting on performance. Yes, I know it's hard to believe, but they are able to do it because they can make poor-performing funds basically disappear—from the perspective of the reporting. If a mutual fund company has a fund that does poorly for a while it simply closes the fund. If it doesn't want to close it, it can merge it with another, and it's as if it never existed and the company doesn't have to report the poor performance. That performance doesn't get factored into the fund into which it merged. The poorly performing fund's track record is wiped away. Remember, it's marketing—it's not truth, it's not full disclosure, and it's not excellence.

This brings us back to Tom saying to himself, "If there are 5,000 mutual funds, how does my broker come up with the best ones for me?" It's called "buying shelf space." The analogy we will use is bread that you buy in the supermarket. As you walk the aisles and come upon the bread section, one brand is right at eye level. Was that just chance, or perhaps the preference of the employee putting out the stock? No, the placement was paid for. The bread company purchased that premium shelf space. Mutual funds do the same. If you want a big brokerage firm to represent your mutual funds, and you've got competition, you make deals. Is it so hard to imagine a mutual fund company, facing loads of competition, approaching the CEO of some big brokerage house and saying, "If you do business with us, here's what we'll do for you"? That indeed is what happens.

Back in 2003, a *BusinessWeek* investigative reporter looked into this practice. His research showed that 99.2 percent of all the mutual funds sales by Smith Barney consisted of mutual funds that paid extra for the privilege of being promoted and marketed to the retail investor. So, it's not about excellence, it's about marketing. To be fair to Smith Barney, they all do this. I wouldn't even call it unethical or wrong, but the public isn't aware of the practice, and the bias inherent in it, although they should be.

Think of it this way: A mutual fund owns stocks. In order to hold Stock A or Stock B, some entity has to purchase those shares and eventually sell them. So if you were, for example, Putnam Investments, and you would like Merrill Lynch to be a purveyor of your fund's shares, you would perhaps tell Merrill Lynch that it is your broker of choice for all internal transactions. Handling all those trades is where Merrill Lynch makes its money. There's nothing illegal in this practice, but knowing this should affect your perception of the mutual fund market. The fund that your broker puts you into is chosen for reasons that have nothing to do with excellence, it's about marketing.

Full disclosure: At one point in my career I was the number-one registered rep in the country. I was responsible for the selection of funds by many average investors. Think of all those discussions I had with retail investors. I would say something like: "Mr. Smith, I've done my due diligence and come to the conclusion that XYZ Fund II is wonderful; this is where we should put your money. Why XYZ Fund II? Because I have looked at the track record of its performance for the past 10 years, and it's been outstanding. It's a highly rated mutual fund with Morningstar. Over the past 10 years it's outperformed virtually all the funds in its category. It's one of the top 10 mutual funds in the entire world, Mr. Smith. I know this because we just happened to have some information on the top 10 mutual funds of the decade, 1990-1999. The average return...I'll even tell you this, of the top 30 funds, 1990-99, the annualized return came to $27.15 million, 27 percent. The best of the lot is XYZ Fund II."

Put yourself in the position of Mr. Smith, listening to this pitch. It's 1999, you retired a year ago, you've worked your whole life, and you've got your nest egg of $1 million, and I say, "Mr. Smith, I'm a financial planner, and I know the ins and outs of this. We don't want to put all of our eggs in one basket. So we'll just put a little bit in each of these funds."

OK, let's fast-forward now to the next decade of 2000–2009. Not one of the funds made the top 1,000 list; the average annual return became a *negative* 4.43 percent. What does that tell you? Remember we talked about the negative sequence of returns? The point being, there's nothing "wrong" with what that broker, like myself, did; it's how we've been "trained" to sell.

It would be nice if all this selecting of mutual funds was done based on objective evaluation and the pure merit of fund performance. But it still wouldn't make much difference, because there is no way to pick funds with any degree of certainty as to what the future will bring. Even the industry says this: "Past performance is not a guarantee of future results." But I think that's often in small type, and I know darn well as a practitioner in this business that financial planners and brokers sell by past performance. They push it and they push Morningstar ratings. And Morningstar itself will tell you, "We have nothing to do with future performance. We grade funds on how they have done relative to their peers."

It strains the imagination to think what a candid, truthful representative of the mutual fund industry would say to Tom about these prospects. The statement would have to be nothing less than, "Tom, Angela, we have no way of picking a mutual fund for you with any proven capability that it will work out in your behalf." That's the case, because of so many factors outside the range of forecasting and projections. It comes down to market movements; when markets move all equities move. Research has shown that with an income-distribution portfolio it doesn't matter if you have strategically diversified among a healthy array of funds. That structuring means very little to performance of the portfolio. It means virtually nothing as to how long that portfolio will last. I go back to the conclusion of the Metropolitan Life study, and the eerie phrase that gets used: "negative sequence of returns." If you start your retirement with the market going up, you'll have a different result than if you start out in the beginning with the market going down. Poor returns in the first years of retirement "cannot be mitigated using any conventional investments for asset-allocation strategy."

The mission of the financial advisor is to present facts clearly so that people can make an informed decision. We're doing our job appropriately if we can help people make smart choices about their money, and increase the likelihood that they can go the distance—in other words, not outlive their money. The greatest threat to the longevity of one's retirement income—other than not saving enough money in the first place—is market fluctuations for the portfolio that is exposed to risk.

The Wall Street system of retirement is not about success; it's about marketing. There's a cost every time you buy and sell a security, so Wall Street doesn't care if you make money, it just wants you buying and selling. That is the goal of Wall Street: for investors to be active. Buy this; sell that. "It's time to move. We now have a better mutual fund," the local office manager tells the salespeople at their Monday morning meeting. "We've got a new mutual fund in to help offset these problems that are going on in the banks." I'm making this up. But we call it the mutual fund du jour. That's what feeds the animal: sales! There are reasons they don't use the word "guaranteed." They talk about investment strategies, but they don't use the word "guaranteed." They don't use the words, "Create yourself a lifetime pension." The insurance industry says that, because that's what it does, and it has the vehicles to do it—which will be explained in-depth later in this book.

SPECIAL RETIREMENT-PLANNING
ADVICE FOR WOMEN

Women face steeper obstacles than men in building a proper invest-ment nest egg. On average women are paid less than men, but their costs of living are not less, so they have less money to save. Research also points out that the typical work life of a woman in a corporation comes to fewer years than a man's. The female life expectancy is greater, which adds to the challenge. When you have fewer years of work, you have fewer years of accumulating pension benefits or your retirement accounts. Lower earnings, lower savings, shorter work tenure, and longer life expectancies—that's a difficult combination of factors to offset.

Advice worth following for the woman in the workplace:

▫ Begin saving now—don't wait until it's too late. Even if you're financially strapped, find a way to "pay yourself first" and put some small amount aside.

▫ Get a financial advisor to calculate what it would take by way of accumulation to have enough assets to create a pension for yourself, one that will allow you to maintain your standard of living. Among some financial planners there is a rule of thumb that retirement living requires 80 percent of your pre-retirement income. And I say, what 20 percent of your life do you want to give up? Especially if you are reading this book, you are likely the type who has conducted her affairs and established a lifestyle that is moderate and prudent. If that's the way you've lived, then you don't have much to cut out. You should plan to create an income that is 100 percent, not 80 percent, of what you've been living on.

▫ Take advantage of the 401(k), especially if your employer is con-tributing. Max out his contribution. That means that the company matches you dollar for dollar, although it will match sometimes up to 4 percent.

Keep up with that match. That's critical, because it's two for one on your money right away.

    □   As you get older, consider an annuity, because it is the only source of lifetime income.

    □   Consider seriously the possibility and requirements of long-term care. That doesn't necessarily mean a nursing home, but long-term care that would cover the costs of a nursing home or in-house care.

CHAPTER 6

HOW TO SELECT A FINANCIAL ADVISOR

I n my practice, we have three tests that we apply to each potential client. The first test or question is: Do we have a good fit, and is there compatibility between client and advisor? Second: Does the prospective client have sufficient assets? (Typically I need at least a quarter of a million dollars of investable assets to take on the client.) Third: Can we add value? And if all three of those are true, then we can have a meaningful relationship.

I do also insist that I be given free rein to protect or, if you will, stand by my recommendations. Sometimes clients will comment: "I feel like you're pressuring me." My response is always the same: "I am pressuring you. That's my job. My job is to move you from A to B if I feel it's in your best interest and I do. And if I am not able to provide the information that will persuade you, I have failed." I believe I have a moral obligation to operate this way.

Make certain that your advisor is not a "yes man." You need someone who will stand his ground and be willing to speak controversially. For your part, you will be responsible for hearing the advisor out and letting him explain himself logically. The advisor has, in my view, a moral obligation, if he or she truly believes that it is in your best interest to move from point A to B, to make that happen. If the advisor backs down just to avoid stress, he has failed in his job and you have failed to take a step that's critical to your future.

For us as financial advisors to habitually acquiesce regarding basic structure of a retirement plan is a discredit to the profession. For example, if a client waves his hand halfway through an explanation by the advisor and says, "No, I don't like the idea of an annuity," and the adviser changes the subject, it's a disservice. At that point he has become a common peddler, an order-taker. And you have to demand that the people around you are not "yes people," that they stand their ground.

I do like the term "advice givers," because I think that so many people are aggressively selling instead of guiding, thus it sets a tone and sets the true professional apart. It should be noted: There is no legal or educational requirement from any state that sets down what you have to do to be a financial advisor or financial planner, and virtually no academic background necessary. This can create a significant gap between real knowledge and your perception of their knowledge. It can lead to a dicey situation. A comparison I use on occasion involves the most dangerous man in Dodge City during frontier times. You could tell him as you walked down the street by his dusty boots and his black hat cocked to one side, carrying his gun belt low on his hip. You moved away. But today, the most dangerous person is dressed in a tailored suit and sits behind a mahogany desk.

Most investment firms run in-house sales training for their new advisors. And some of these run for several weeks. But while they're being conducted, the rookies are expected to be prospecting and closing sales. And finally, when their training ends, these people have been indoctrinated into the company's way and are able to give "expert" advice. Therefore, they learn the company's way and the company's products. Part of the training teaches them to say, "Even though we're employed by XYZ Financial, we are able to access virtually any financial product. We truly are an impartial source of information."

However, when that company has a sales contest with a week's vacation in Cancun or the Virgin Islands as the prize, the contest rules never say: "Build your sales for the period using virtually any financial product." The rules say: "At least one third of all sales must be company-endorsed vehicles." The pressure is on the people who work in the local offices of these big Wall Street companies. They are expected to win investors over to the company's sponsored in-house products or to the mutual fund that paved their way to get in. Their health care, their pensions, everything is tied to the sale of these company products. It's so much smoke and mirrors. If you're dealing with a big firm, it's like going to a restaurant and not being presented part of the menu.

I tell a story about the couple who went to the same restaurant night after night, year after year, and always had the same waiter. One night, though, their waiter wasn't there. And the husband said, "I'm really not happy with the choices we've had, and I just don't know what to order tonight." The waiter said, "Well open your menu." The man opened his menu and the waiter said, "No, open it all the way." It was a tri-fold menu. The man finally laid eyes on that third flap, and a whole new world opened.

My concern with the brokerage industry is that in this world, with asset classes 1, 2, and 3, most brokerage firms use a tri-fold menu and you are never exposed to class 3. You need to find an advisor who has access to all the tools, to everything that would be on the world menu. Therefore, if you don't own something, it's because you made an informed decision not to have this in your portfolio. It is not because you didn't know it existed or it was misrepresented.

Another thing I encourage on my radio show is for people to listen to their intuition. Your financial advisor may be much less educated than you think. And also he or she is not necessarily in a better position to make financial decisions than you are. If you're a married man, take your wife to all appointments. Even if she's not a financial person, women have been given, for the most part, a greater sense of intuition than men. And if there's a nagging feeling inside that you don't like this person or don't feel right about the recommendation, listen to what your wife has to say. Her intuition could be more important than all your statistical understanding.

I have another caution while we're talking about education. Be cautious about your CPA or your attorney giving financial advice. Attorneys have literally zero training in this field. And accountants are trained to put numbers in boxes and to add and to know about debits and credits. They are not, for the most part, trained in financial vehicles. And they are not, by training, capable of serving as financial advice givers.

There are a lot of egos out there. Yes there are many instances of clients who trust their attorney or their accountant because they perform well in their specialties. Your trust in them as lawyers or accountants does not mean that these people are going to be able to give good counsel when it comes to your long-term financial plans. That's just a warning. I'm not trying to put these people down; I'm trying to put them in perspective.

There's a difference between the accumulation specialist who makes up 99.9 percent of all advisors and the retirement manager. Retirement portfolios need to be managed in a different fashion than an accumulation portfolio, and you need a retirement management specialist. If the advice that your broker is giving you is the same advice he's giving some 50-year-old or 45-year-old, you've got the wrong guy.

It's important to express your specific investment desires and fears to your advisor. And then it is important to ask your advisor what his philosophical approach is to the handling of you as a pre- or existing retiree? In all likelihood you will be the first one to ever ask him that question.

If the person's eyes become glazed over in what I call the dead-trout stare, and it looks as if he is now thinking on his feet, you might want to exit the room. But if he says yes, I do have a philosophy about managing retirees' money, hear him out. For example, here is one of mine: If an individual tells me that he cannot afford to lose money in a particular segment of his assets, I will never expose those assets to the risk of market loss.

I will make mistakes, but I have made a commitment not to expose your assets to a big mistake. We have two questions on each investment decision. Would this decision expose me to a big mistake, or would this decision expose my assets to a little mistake? Say somebody tells me, "I cannot afford to lose money. I do not want to lose money for whatever reason; I've worked too hard. I just can't afford to go backward." If I were to place that client's funds in a vehicle that had complete safety of principle and the market went up and we missed it, we could say we just missed making some money. The market went up 9 percent and we only made 5 percent. Is that a big mistake? Is that a little mistake? Weigh it against a case in which we had gone into the market and it went down 30 percent and we lost 30 percent. Is that a big mistake or a little mistake?

And if you deem the latter to be a big mistake and the former to be a small mistake, that would be the road we would travel. We know we can't always be right, but we will not expose our assets to a big mistake. That's my number-two philosophy.

So you need to match philosophies. Does his philosophy match yours? And then if it appears that it does, have him recap the conversation—his understanding of your goals and objectives and fears and his philosophies—and put it forth in writing on his letterhead and submit to you. This is not child's play. This is about somebody's largest asset. It has to be managed at this level of professionalism and care. And if the person on the other side of the table doesn't want to do it, get out of the room.

Also make sure that the individual is experienced, not just book-smart.

Besides experience, you need to consider age-appropriateness. If you're a 60-year-old and you're sitting in front of a 35-year-old who has an MBA and was trained by his brokerage, he's probably a very smart person but has no idea what it's like to be 60 years old and what the loss 20 percent of your wealth could do to you emotionally. It's no skin off them if they lose. I think it makes sense for seniors to do business with seniors. People who have been in the arena are their best guides.

And next, does this advisor possess a full array of tools? Remember, you want to make sure that you see the whole menu, not just two of the three folds. Because the reality is, you're going to get advice only on what his company has to offer. And if they don't have information on a product you ask about, it will either be dismissed as irrelevant or maligned and diminished. You're going to get advice on only those tools he has placed in his tool belt.

You have to know that it's not your broker's fault. He or she works in a closed world after going through the company training. These brokers are loyal to their companies. They're not exposed to alternative thinking and options. They're often intentionally misinformed by their sales trainers. Look, a sales trainer gets paid on how much in commissions his people put together, and they often just don't have a full tool belt. And then some of the tool manufacturers pay extra money so that certain tools will be pushed.

I feel the true strength of somebody coming to my firm is that I don't have anybody in New York telling me what's best for my clients. My rent is not subsidized. My health care insurance is not subsidized by any carrier. Nothing. My bookkeeper writes the check for my rent, for health insurance. It's more expensive to run my businesses in this manner, but it allows me to speak the truth to individuals. And I'm one of very few. We are a minority. And I think it's a very powerful consumer factor.

The final consideration is whether your advisor has the ability to coordinate his work with your accountant and your attorney. This is the full team, and I call myself the quarterback. You, as the client, are well-served to have your financial advisor, your attorney and your accountant in communication with one another. Ideally, we are working and discussing your situation regarding investments, taxes and estate planning.

In your search for an effective financial advisor, here are five important questions to ask:

1. Do you specialize as a retirement income manager?
2. How do you do that differently than for your other portfolios or for your other clients?
3. Are you certified as a planning expert?
4. Are you an author? Have you written anything on the subject on which you counsel?
5. Do you invest in ongoing professional knowledge?

If you receive solid answers to these questions, you are on the way to selecting an advisor who will work successfully on your behalf.

CHAPTER 7

THE INSURANCE SYSTEM OF RETIREMENT

T om found himself staring into a dark corner of the room, brooding once again over 10 years of market turbulence, economic crisis, and the fact that he had never been offered a means of building wealth slowly while avoiding risk. Anger was flowing over him. And he questioned what other opportunities he might have missed. What might a lack of full information or even distorted, biased information have cost him and other American investors? Tom thought how important it is to find good help. How could he find an advisor who had knowledge, expertise, and the full capability—or access to all the various products?

The Wall Street system of retirement is based on greed, promises, old ideas and defunct strategies. The insurance system of retirement is based on integrity, guarantees and certainty. It's a secure system of retirement.

The annuities that have been available for more than 100 years provide more features than virtually any other investments. Investors can rely on the safety of the insurance industry, with its mandated reserve requirements, financial clout, and the vigilance of truly effective outside rating agencies. No one has ever lost a dime in a fixed annuity. The safety record of this conservative investment vehicle is unequalled. When you purchase a fixed rate "hybrid" annuity your principle is guaranteed, your earnings are tied to an index like the S&P 500, and your gains become locked in on each policy anniversary.

When you deposit a dollar in a bank account, the bank by law has to keep a certain amount on reserve. That amount depends upon the type of account, but it ranges from zero to 10 cents. When you purchase a fixed annuity, the insurance company by law must set aside more than a dollar in reserves. The insurer could use these excess reserves only to settle withdrawals and redemptions. The money cannot be used to settle insurance claims, pay overhead, settle bad debts, or take care of any other nonrelated annuity item. During the Great Depression it was not the U.S. government that bailed out all the insolvent banks. It was the insurance industry.

If there were ever a financial collapse in the United States, the insurance industry would be the second-to-last entity to fold (second only to the government). Additionally, each state has a guarantee association whose purpose is to back up any potentially insolvent insurance carrier. They were all founded by the individual states' legislatures to protect life and annuity insurance policyholders and their beneficiaries. It does not matter where the insurance company is headquartered—every state mandates that all companies doing business within the state sign an agreement to abide by the state's laws and requirements. To operate these guarantee associations, they take a small percentage of every annuity and every dollar of insurance coverage. That payment is called a premium tax.

If you have never heard of the state guarantee association, I'm not surprised, because agents are prohibited from explaining it to prospective customers (as counterproductive as this may sound). Sometime when you are thinking about future income security, look up the website of the National Organization of Life and Health Insurance Guaranty Associations at www.nolhga.com/.

Obviously every policyholder is protected by the full faith and credit of the issuing corporation. Then it is further backed up by that state fund. If that state fund then becomes insufficient to cover whatever shortfall exists, the state has the authority, under its NOLHGA, to assess every company that does business in the state and pro-rate their share of the deficiency. So the guarantee is a real guarantee. It's way beyond the financial ability of the company. There is no government bailout of an insurance company—they are forced by law to bail each other out.

The insurance companies' reserve requirements are anything but partial. That makes them different from banks. If you deposited $100,000 in Chase Bank today, it has to keep 10 cents from every dollar on hand in reserves. It can take 90 cents and go to the Fed to borrow nine times that. So if you gave the bank $1 million, it has to set aside $100,000. It can go to the Federal Reserve and borrow $900,000 – then take that money and make whatever frivolous loan it chooses. That's why you and I bail the banks out. Do you see the leverage of a bank?

With the insurance industry, if you give a company $1 million, it has to add 10 percent of its own money on top of it for a total of $1.1 million. And of that, it will put 85 percent to 90 percent in Treasuries and high-grade corporate bonds. There's no leveraging there. There's a completely different financial structure and integrity.

The insurance industry is built on integrity, safety and security. And the banking industry and Wall Street are built on leverage and greed.

Let's be candid. If your broker or financial advisor doesn't carry something, how quick will he or she be to recommend it? Additionally, many financial planners charge fees for their "expert guidance." The hybrid plan requires no guidance. It's an automated system, free of any and all fees, because there are no changes being made all the time you own it. It's an investment haven, with fine potential for growth based on safety and security. What's the likelihood of it being recommended by your "expert"?

This is an opportunity you need to investigate. For the investors who become involved with it, peace of mind and a valid sense of hope come with the package. It's a world of safety and growth opportunity. It may not fit for you, but it merits your knowing its details. If you end up not owning a hybrid, let it be because you choose not to, not because you didn't know about it or your advisor dismissed it as irrelevant or not for you, very possibly because it subverts his own business model.

We have learned throughout this book that the main determinants of a portfolio's success are external, mainly negative returns and inflation—items that a broker or financial advisor has no control over. Asset allocation and diversification had been shown not to have a major impact on portfolios. Therefore, the key to having a successful future is not what you can do with the portfolio, but with your assets.

For example, you must select an asset that is exempt from the external factors of a portfolio's failure—market loss and inflation. I have found but one asset in the world designed to meet and beat those problems. *It is the fixed-index, hybrid annuity.* Exempt from market loss, it has the opportunity to fight inflation and the ability to generate a lifetime income. It is as close to a perfect investment as I could imagine or have ever seen. I encourage you to get the full facts.

There are three safe-haven investments: Certificates of deposit offered by banks, U.S. Treasury bonds, and annuities purchased from insurance companies.

First of all, what is an annuity? It is a contract between a person, called an annuitant, and an insurance company. Principal is guaranteed, interest is credited, and the rate of return is based on the type of annuity chosen. The four types are:

- Immediate
- Fixed
- Variable
- Fixed-index, or hybrid, annuity

An **immediate annuity** is like a pension. The annuitant makes a one-time payment (premium) to the insurance company. The premium, or principal, is totally guaranteed. The insurance company pays a periodic stream of payments to the annuitant (normally beginning within one year), until death

It offers multiple payout options:

- Single-pay—pays for the life of the annuitant.
- Joint and survivor—payouts are made as long as both spouses are alive.
- Life-and-period-certain—a fancy name that simply means the minimum period the payments will be made. This is an important feature that I recommend be looked at on all immediate annuities, though it has pros and cons.

On the pro side, you are guaranteed principal, reliable stream of lifetime income, elimination of market risk, and elimination of longevity risk. In other words, with a life-and-period-certain annuity, you receive a reliable income for life. On the con side, the insurance keeps any excess principal monies.

The next two types of annuities, fixed and variable, are known as **deferred annuities**.

A fixed-rate deferred annuity, very much resembling a bank certificate of deposit, is very simple. Principal is guaranteed; likewise, the interest rate is fixed and guaranteed for a certain period of time. At the end of the guarantee period, the annuity can be renewed higher or lower based on current interest rates, or cancelled without penalty. All interest income tax is deferred, and it can be moved to a new annuity without incurring taxes. If it is cancelled and not rolled into a new annuity, ordinary income taxes will be applied to the earnings.

Variable deferred annuities are like mutual funds. The interest on these plans varies. Principal is not guaranteed; it can increase and decrease based on the performance of the underlying mutual funds. Let me say here that as a result of the market crashes in the 2000s, insurance companies have come up with all kinds of options to guarantee the monies inside variable annuities. However, these options have a price tag. Within variable annuities, the fees charged typically range from 2½ percent to 5 percent.

Example: A $100,000 investment could incur $5,000 a year in fees. Over the last 10 years, in which the market made no money and most variable annuity holders made no money, the companies would have made $50,000 in fees. These fees are charged regardless of gains or losses. Variable annuities are evolving, with more features and options, each of which have a price tag of which the investor must be aware. Details on these costs can be obtained within the prospectus, some of which are longer than 300 pages.

I have a client who in September of 2010 entered into a variable annuity contract and he brought it in to show me. In the prospectus we found the page with the fee schedule. If the maximum fees were applied where Prudential said it could do so—and virtually all the companies are moving in that direction—over a 10-year period on that $10,000 investment, my client will have paid $6,000-plus in fees. That's in my office, in the top drawer. I read it, I underlined it, it's in my desk, and any client who wants to take a look at it can drop by any time.

The variable annuity is a product of the 1970s. It was designed when income tax rates were much higher than today and capital gains were taxed at ordinary income rates. Variable annuities were designed for high-income-tax-bracket individuals—primarily traders, people who liked to buy and sell. The instrument gave them a place to tax-defer their earnings. The vehicle's cost of 2 percent to 5 percent was inconsequential if individuals were sheltering their gains from very high income taxes. The problem is that many people owning these today are not high-income, high-tax-bracket individuals.

As a matter of fact, most variable annuities that I review are held by individuals in their IRAs which have zero tax bracket. Therefore, they have taken a tax deferred vehicle called a variable annuity with high fees of two to five percent and put it in a tax deferred vehicle. No leading expert in America condones this. Jane Bryant Quinn of *Newsweek* says she would like to smash all variable annuities to smithereens. Suze Orman states that the variable annuity is number one on her "hate list." The AARP, along with *Money* magazine and many other respected periodicals all condemn this practice. It seems to me the only ones who proclaim it to be a good idea are the brokerage firms that sell it.

Caution: Do not purchase a variable annuity for your IRA without examining other alternatives.

For some variable annuities, you can buy a guaranteed minimum income benefit—GMIB—in which you pay the insurance carrier extra money to guarantee a stated rate of growth on a separate fund. It's simply a bookkeeping account from which you could draw an income, normally after one year. Example: Assume a principal of $100,000. It could fall to $50,000 in five years, while your guaranteed minimum income benefit—a hypothetical—has grown to, let's say, $125,000. You cannot access the principal of that $125,000 you can only access the income—typically 5 percent per year.

As a radio host, speaking to callers about their investing experiences, I find that variable annuities are the number-one misunderstood vehicle. People e-mail my show, call my show, stating that they have an investment with ABC variable annuity and they were guaranteed a 5 percent return. What they don't understand is that it is a 5 percent return on their *income* account. If the market goes down, the balance on their base, or principal amount, goes down.

If you ever needed your lump sum of money, perhaps for a medical issue, you'd have to take it from your reduced principal account, you see? It is the most misunderstood investment I have ever experienced, and I want to take a stand. The communication is the responsibility of the advice-giver, not the client, and if I find the overwhelming majority of individuals that I speak to misunderstand this product, I have to believe that it is being misrepresented.

Why would anyone, knowing this information, take this action? The answer is that brokerage firms and many financial planners—to hark back to Russ' Rules—don't carry the product that is vastly superior to the variable annuity, which is the hybrid annuity, or fixed-index annuity. The hybrid, which we're going to talk about next, is not carried by any brokerage firm in America, period. Therefore, they don't even have it to sell, so what do you think they're going to do? They're going to either keep it under wraps or diminish it. That's been their disinformation campaign.

I'm just cynical enough to believe that it could be because it doesn't meet their profit needs. Why else? Wall Street is transaction-driven—buy the stock, buy the bond, sell the stock, sell the bond. Variable annuities—what is it that's inside them? Mutual funds. Transactions. Each of which generates a fee. Over the past 10 years the only people to make money in variable annuities has been the agent or the representative and Wall Street, certainly not the consumer. If you were to ask me what is the number-one thing Wall Street wants Americans to do, I would tell you that it wants them to buy and sell so the firms are always creating some type of statements as to why investors should leave mutual fund A or go into mutual fund B, even if it's a lateral move.

Are there positives to the variable annuity? To stretch fairness, it could be said that the positive would be market potential—exposure to market upside. The negatives are many: downside risk to principle, expensive fees, limited liquidity, and surrender periods. The surrender period is that time required by the insurance company over which the contract runs. If surrendered prior to the end of the period, a charge is typically assessed. In other words, the annuitant is charged if he or she decides to end the annuity before the term of its life. I have not found a single leading expert who recommends variable annuities in an IRA.

This brings us to the investment you truly need to know about, the **fixed-index annuity**.

The fixed-index annuity is sometimes referred to as a hybrid because it combines some of the best features of the fixed, immediate and variable into one plan.

The fixed-index annuity gets my endorsement as the near-perfect retirement funding and income vehicle. I think of it as the gold standard for retirees. Hybrid annuities are designed and targeted for people ages 45 to 75, those headed for or already in retirement. They offer what most retirees are seeking: safety. First, the principal is exempt from market loss. Second, you get a chance to beat inflation. And third, you tap it to provide yourself an income—immediate or deferred—that you cannot outlive. It's the single greatest weapon to defeat these three major threats to a successful retirement—market loss, increasing costs of living, and longevity.

Here's how this product works. An individual makes a payment to an insurance company. Principal is guaranteed exactly as it is in the fixed annuity, and interest is determined by automatically capturing market gains when financial markets go up. In most cases, it is tied to the S&P 500 or another index. Gains become "locked in" annually, and when markets go down, there is no loss in account value. The effect is that you were treading water in that particular period. Gains are protected. They become part of the principal. But

in a down year you go neither up nor down. The net account difference in that down market is zero.

This gives rise to the saying, "Zero is your hero." In a year when
Wall Street investors take losses, you don't. You cannot tolerate
market loss in a retirement or distribution portfolio. You can go
up; you can go sideways; but you cannot go backward. This is a
vehicle that I feel has been misrepresented and maligned by Wall
Street, perhaps because it is not profitable enough. I cannot find one
Wall Street firm that carries it in its inventory. Seniors need to know
of its existence.

In a personal finance policy brief published by the Wharton
Financial Institutions Center, Dr. David F. Babbel and colleagues
examined actual contracts and returns from fixed-index annuities
from 18 carriers from 1997 through 2005. The first finding is that
fixed-income annuity returns have been competitive with alternative portfolios of stocks and bonds. They have achieved respectable
returns in robust markets. Here's an excerpt from the study:

> Studies that have made negative comments on fixed-index
> annuities have been based upon assumptions and not on realities.
> When actual returns are utilized, conclusions are markedly
> different. Performance—based on five-year annual returns
> 1997 through 2007—the fixed-index annuities averaged 5.79
> percent per year. Based upon 141 actual five-year periods,
> 1995-2009, real-world purchases of fixed-indexed annuities
> have outperformed the S&P 500 67 percent of the time.

Think of this: an alternative to Wall Street; safety, opportunity
and income that cannot be outlived; yet has outperformed the stock
market 67 percent of the time. Many financial planners don't like
these plans. Brokers don't have them. Financial planners who sell

securities can't charge their management fees if you own one of these. The fixed-index annuity is shaking up Wall Street and shaking up the financial planning industry.

As an early champion of this investment format, I received blank looks, rolled eyes and dismissive criticism. To the critics, I would let the German philosopher Arthur Schopenhauer offer the proper refutation. It was Schopenhauer, writing in the early 19th century, who penned this assertion: "All truth passes through three stages. First, it is ridiculed. Second, it is violently opposed. Third, it is accepted as being self-evident." That observation is slowly being reflected in the changing public and professional view of fixed-index hybrid annuities.

The new gold standard for investing has been created, it is here, and it does work. You do not have to risk your assets in order for the opportunity to grow your money. I call it reward without risk.

Note: These annuities are not variable annuities, which I and most leading experts deplore. It takes on the greatest single danger to the successful retirement, loss of principal, so states Jim Otar in his excellent textbook, Unveiling the Retirement Myths.

According to Mr. Otar, a loss of 10 percent in the first years of retirement can shorten a portfolio life by 10 to 15 years. A retiree must avoid losses and now, for the first time, there is a vehicle available. Is it perfect? No, but thousands of people are finding that this is the right retirement funding vehicle to defeat the three beasts of retirement, loss of principal, increased cost of living, and outliving one's money. There's no guessing, it's simply math. Markets are up, you share. Markets are down, you tread water. Ask yourself, would you give up some of the upside of the market to have no exposure to the down? If yes, you owe it to yourself to investigate this vehicle.

The initial, fundamental advantage is you have no exposure to market loss. Then there is the wonderful advantage that you've got a bona fide opportunity for gain. Along with that, it's an exemplary vehicle for providing lifetime income. As for fees, you will find there are either no fees or else very low fees, depending on your selection of investment characteristics. Finally, there is the great advantage of safety of principal: Gains are locked in, and you won't go backward from the point that you've moved up to. The only notable disadvantage is that your gains will be more limited in a solid, extended bull market for stocks. For the great majority of people, that's a deal they like and one they gladly take.

One more thing…add on's

An add on is known as a RIDER. A rider is an extra option that can be added to the BASE vehicle. The most common is an INCOME RIDER, referred to as a guaranteed minimum withdrawal benefit (GMWB).

The GMWB grows at a stated rate (normally 6%-8%) per year and is available to provide a minimum source of retirement income from a guaranteed base. Its cost typically runs .40 to .95 per year and typically comes with a bonus of 8% to 10% on your initial contribution. For example: male age 60 and has $200,000 + 8% (bonus) = $216,000 @ 7%/per year. In 10 years = $393,430.

At age 70 this plan will produce nearly $ 26,000 per year for your life and your spouse (Joint life). Note: These are withdrawals, not annuitization, as such you remain in control of your money. You can stop and restart at any time. This payout is based upon your age and runs between 5% and 8% per year. Also if anything remains in the base contract at the second death the balance is passed on to your heirs.

With some companies there are also health care benefits included. Example: the same $200,000 + 8%= $216,000 @ 7%/per year= $393,400. Lifetime Income (joint life) = $26,000. If there is a medical issue and care is needed- at home or otherwise- the company will "double" the amount of payments for five years ($50,000/year) and still keep their promise of LIFETIME payout for both parties. Note, there is typically a 24 month waiting period prior to beginning this benefit.

No doubt, you can see the benefits that some of these riders hold.

A note of caution—the devil is in the details. There are more than 150 fixed-index annuities. Not all of these hybrids are alike. There are many nuances, and your choice will depend upon the objectives and when income might be needed. Our firm, along with others with whom we partner, have looked at virtually all of them and only seven have come through our consumer filters. Get with an advisor you know and trust, even on this exemplary investment vehicle.

APPENDIX

APPENDIX

Determine Your Risk Profile and Investment Objectives

The first step in the Asset Management Process is to know yourself and determine your investor profile or personality. This will help define important factors such as your risk tolerance, return objectives, and your time horizon.

This profile will help build the base of information needed for you to progress to the next step in the asset management process— the development of an appropriate strategy.

To complete this profile, answer each question with a sentence or two or by circling the letter that best matches your personal situation.

KNOWING YOURSELF

1. How do you feel about your current investments?

2. When making an investment, what are your biggest fears? (Number in order of priority, with 1 the highest and 4 the lowest.)
- a. ( ) Losing money
- b. ( ) Not being told everything
- c. ( ) Not knowing the risks
- d. ( ) Not really understanding and not feeling comfortable asking more questions.

3. Which is more important?
- a. Safety of the money invested
- b. Staying ahead of inflation

4. Is it your belief that growth-oriented investments typically…
- a. Rise steadily
- b. Fluctuate up and down yet, over an extended period of three to five years, normally have a gain

5. How would you feel about an investment that fluctuates in value?

6. How would you describe your understanding of various investments? (Circle one.)

I have a very good understanding about these concepts.

I have a fair understanding of these concepts.

I know very little about these concepts.

I know nothing about these concepts

GUIDE TO FINANCIAL AWARENESS - Circle your choices

Degree of Understanding	Understand Well	Understand Little
Certificates of Deposits	1 2 3 4 5	1 2 3 4 5
Government Bonds	1 2 3 4 5	1 2 3 4 5
Individual Stocks	1 2 3 4 5	1 2 3 4 5
Mutual Funds	1 2 3 4 5	1 2 3 4 5
Tax-Deferred Mutual Funds	1 2 3 4 5	1 2 3 4 5
Fixed Annuities	1 2 3 4 5	1 2 3 4 5
Fixed-Index Annuities	1 2 3 4 5	1 2 3 4 5
Variable Annuities	1 2 3 4 5	1 2 3 4 5
Real Estate Investment Trusts	1 2 3 4 5	1 2 3 4 5
Diversification	1 2 3 4 5	1 2 3 4 5
Asset Allocation	1 2 3 4 5	1 2 3 4 5

Which of the following do you consider the main obstacles to achieving your financial goals? Prioritize three.

    a. Lack of overall plan

    b. Inflation

    c. Fear of outside advice

    d. Market losses

    e. Longevity

    f. Health-care expenses

INVESTMENT OBJECTIVES

1. Which of the following best describes your investment objectives?

    a. Preserving principal

    b. Chance to beat inflation

    c. Creating stable and predictable lifetime income

    d. Growing my assets substantially

2. Prioritize financial goals

	Least		Concerned		Most
Income in retirement	1	2	3	4	5
Managing my retirement	1	2	3	4	5
Inflation's effect on my retirement	1	2	3	4	5
The adequacy of my nest egg	1	2	3	4	5
The financial risk of a nursing home	1	2	3	4	5
My spouse's security in the event of my premature death					
	1	2	3	4	5
Reducing income taxes	1	2	3	4	5
Protecting my assets from loss	1	2	3	4	5
Other	1	2	3	4	5

TIME HORIZON

1. What is the time frame for you to achieve your financial goals?
   a. 0–5 years
   b. 5–10 years
   c. 10–15 years
   d. 15 years or longer

2. Five years from now, what do you expect your standard of living to be?
   a. The same as it is now
   b. Somewhat better than it is now
   c. Substantially better than it is now

3. Ten years from now, what do you expect your portfolio value to be?

    a. The same or a little greater than it is today

    b. Moderately greater than it is today

    c. Substantially greater than it is today

4. What is your current income requirement from this portfolio?

    a. More than 4

    b. 2 to 4

    c. 0 to 2

5. What do you want to do with the income generated by your portfolio?

    a. Receive all income

    b. Receive some and reinvest some

    c. Reinvest all income

6. Do you believe it is prudent to position a percentage of your assets into vehicles that are exempt from market downturns?

    Yes   No   Uncertain

7. If yes, do you have a percentage in mind?

    Consider the "rule of 100" 100-age = risk

    For example, 100-65 = 35, or 65 percent safe, 35 percent risk

8. What would you consider a reasonable rate of return?

9. For the rate of return that you have indicated, please select the item that you feel most appropriately identifies the risk level necessary to achieve your objectives.

      a. ( ) I'm really not sure
      b. ( ) Low risk
      c. ( ) Moderate risk
      d. ( ) Moderate-to-aggressive risk
      e. ( ) Aggressive risk

RISK TOLERANCE

1. Which statement best describes your investment objectives?

      a. ( ) I am willing to assume a low level of risk in an effort to keep pace with inflation.
      b. ( ) I am willing to assume a moderate level of risk in an effort to stay ahead of inflation.
      c. ( ) I am willing to assume a substantial level of risk in an effort to significantly outpace inflation.

2. If you could potentially get a higher rate of return by increasing the risk on your investment you would (select one):

      a. ( ) Accept a lot more risk with all your money
      b. ( ) Accept slightly more risk with some of your money
      c. ( ) Not accept any more risk

3. Which of the following statements best describes what your reaction would be if the value of your portfolio suddenly declined 15 percent?

      a. ( ) I would be very concerned because I cannot accept fluctuations in the value of my portfolio.

b. ( ) If the amount of income I received was unaffected, it would not bother me.

c. ( ) I invest for long-term growth but would be concerned about even a temporary change.

d. ( ) I invest for long-term growth and accept temporary changes due to market fluctuation.

What to Do After the Death
or Disability of a Spouse

The death or serious disability of your spouse is a traumatic event. Dealing with the event, your own feelings, and those of your family can result in overlooked details and additional confusion.

The following checklist is designed to help you get through the details as easily as possible. The suggestions are general and should be adapted to your particular situation through conferences with your family and with legal and financial advisors.

CHECKLIST

1. If you are alone, telephone a friend or relative who can spend the next few hours with you. Shock and trauma can take unexpected forms.

2. Locate the family's important papers. Gather as many as possible, and continue to do so for the next few weeks.

3. Be aware that certain jointly held assets, such as safe-deposit boxes and joint checking or savings accounts, may be frozen as soon as the institution involved becomes aware that one of the joint owners has died. Although such assets are intended to pass to the surviving spouse outside the normal probate process, actual possession may be delayed pending a court order releasing them. The order may depend on proving to inheritance or estate tax officials that the estate owns other assets adequate to pay potential estate or inheritance tax.

4. Notify a funeral director and make an appointment to discuss arrangements. Request several copies of your

spouse's death certificate, which you'll need for your spouse's employer, life insurance companies, and legal procedures.

5. Notify your attorney. Make an appointment to review your spouse's will and to discuss state and federal death taxes that are payable.

6. Notify your state office for inheritance tax, which will be listed in the phone book under the state if you live in an urban area. If you do not, your funeral director can provide the proper address. Ask for the required forms. In many states you must have a release from the state inheritance tax office before company or insurance benefits can be paid.

7. Telephone your spouse's employee benefits office with the following information: your spouse's name, Social Security number, date of death, whether the death was due to accident or illness, and your name and address. The company can begin processing benefits immediately.

8. If your spouse was eligible for Medicare, notify your program office and provide the same information as listed in #7

9. Notify life or accident insurers of your spouse's death. Give the same information as listed in #7 and ask what further information is needed to begin processing your claim. Ask which payment option your spouse has elected, and select another option if you would so prefer. If there are no payment options you will be paid in a lump sum.

10. Notify your Social Security office of the death. Claims may be expedited if you go in person to the nearest office to sign a claim for survivor's benefits. Look for the address under U.S. Government in the phone book.

11. If you need emergency cash before insurance claims are paid, a cash advance might be made for any life insurance benefits to which you are entitled.

12. If your spouse was ever in the service, notify the Veterans Administration. You may be eligible for death or disability benefits.

13. Record in a small ledger all the money you spend. These figures will be needed for tax returns.

GENERAL DEFINITIONS

ASSET ALLOCATION

An investment strategy that attempts to balance risk and reward by adjusting the percentage of each asset in an investment portfolio according to the investor's risk tolerance, goals, and investment time frame.

ANNUITY

An investment contract usually purchased from an insurance company that will provide the purchaser (annuitant) with future payments at regular intervals or a lump-sum payout. If the annuitant dies during the payout period, the remaining benefits are paid to the named beneficiary.

Fixed annuity: The insurance company invests the purchaser's principal in fixed-income instruments (bonds, mortgages, etc.) and guarantees the principal and a minimum payout.

Fixed-index annuity (FIA): A type of annuity that grows at the greater of a) an annual guaranteed minimum rate of return; or b) the return from a specified stock market index (such as the S&P 500), reduced by certain expenses and formulas. At the time the contract is opened, a term is chosen, which is the number of years until the principal is guaranteed and the surrender period is finished. Over the past decade, FIAs, while safe, have out-produced the S&P 500, Dow Jones Industrial Average, and the NASDAQ.

Variable annuity: The insurance company invests the purchaser's principal in equities (common stock) and neither principal nor payout is guaranteed.

NOTE: Some companies allow purchasers to split their principal between fixed and variable components. Funds placed in an annuity accumulate and compound tax-free until they are withdrawn. At withdrawal, part of the payout is considered return of principal and is exempt from tax. Annuities can be purchased by a single payment or through periodic installments.

BEAR MARKET

A market condition in which the prices of securities are falling, and widespread pessimism causes the negative sentiment to be self-sustaining. As investors anticipate losses in a bear market and selling continues, pessimism only grows. Although figures can vary, for many, a downturn of 20 percent or more in multiple broad market indexes, such as the Dow Jones Industrial Average or S&P 500, over at least a two-month period, is considered an entry into a bear market.

BLUE CHIP STOCK

Stock of a well-established and financially sound company that has demonstrated its ability to pay dividends in both good and bad times. These stocks are usually less risky than others. The stock price of a blue chip usually closely follows the S&P 500.

BONDS (Also see LOANER)

They are certificates of debt. When you buy bonds, you are lending money. They are issued by a government entity or a corporation, which guarantees payment of the original investment plus interest by a specified future date. Thus, bonds are referred to as fixed-dollar investments because their yield is predetermined. They are guaranteed as to principal if assets are available at maturity, or as to rate of return if funds are available. They are not guaranteed to grow, regardless of any increase in the profits of the issuing corporation.

Corporate bonds are normally rated according to credit worthiness —AAA bonds are the most secure. The yields are primarily influenced by overall interest rates and the creditworthiness of the issuing company. In general, the higher the grade, the lower the yield.

Convertible bonds are corporate bonds that are convertible into common stock. They offer a chance for capital appreciation if the price of the underlying common stock rises, and generally their current yield is higher than the dividend return on the common stock.

Government bonds are backed by the federal, state or municipal government issuing them.

Zero coupon bonds come in several forms: Treasury zeros, corporate zeros or municipal zeros. These vehicles function as automatic compounding machines. They do not pay any interest (zero) and are sold at a fraction of what their face value (full value) will be at maturity. They allow an investor to lock into a future return that is wholly predictable, that is, assuming the issue does not default.

NOTE: You have to pay taxes each year on the accrued interest even though you do not have it. This provision makes zeros most suitable for Keoghs, IRAs and other tax-deferred savings plans.

BULL MARKET

A prolonged period in which investment prices rise faster than their historical average. Bull markets can happen as a result of an economic recovery, an economic boom, or investor psychology. The longest and most famous bull market is the one that began in the early 1990s in which the U.S. equity markets grew at their fastest pace ever. Opposite of a bear market.

CAPITAL (Sometimes referred to as PRINCIPAL)

The actual amount of money that you invest. If, for example, you buy shares of a mutual fund for $500, that amount is your capital investment.

CAPITAL APPRECIATION OR GROWTH

The increase in or market value of an investment over and above the purchase price.

CONSUMER PRICE INDEX (CPI)

The standard measure of change in the price of goods and services. Note: Social Security checks are based on the CPI. If the index rises 3 percent or more in a year, next year's Social Security benefits will rise 3 percent or more.

CERTIFICATE OF DEPOSIT (CD)

A receipt issued by a bank for a cash deposit for a specified period of time (a week to several years) at a fixed rate of interest. At maturity the bank pays the principal plus all accumulated interest. Generally CDs offer a better pretax return than money funds, but you forego some liquidity. Used for parking cash over longer periods. CDs come in standard maturities of three, six, nine and 12 months. The federal government insures both principal and interest up to $100,000 per person.

Negotiable CDs may be transferred before maturity.

Nonnegotiable CDs are not readily transferred, and early withdrawals are subject to Interest penalties.

NOTE: Although there are substantial penalties for early withdrawal, CDs are tax deductible.

COLLECTIBLES/TANGIBLES/HARD ASSETS

These assets hold the promise of some protection from the ravages of inflation. Included in this group are gold and silver bullion and coins, rare gold and silver coins, junk silver coins, colored gemstones, rare stamps, and mutual funds that invest in gold stocks.

NOTE: These assets have historically done well when the mood of the economy was bleak and uncertain. Be aware that tangibles and collectibles do not yield interest or dividends. Their value depends on future price appreciation.

COMMODOTIES

A generic term for goods such as grain, foodstuffs, livestock, oils and metals traded on national exchanges.

DIVERSIFICATION

One of the major methods of reducing risk in investing. When you diversify, you spread your investment over a number of different securities and types of investments.

DIVIDENDS

A distribution to shareholders of income earned by individual securities and mutual funds.

DOLLAR COST AVERAGING

Investing a *fixed amount* of money at regular *intervals* in either equity mutual (common stock) funds or individual stocks. This results in lowering the average price of the security below the average market price per share over the investment period. It works! This is a long-term investment technique that mathematically beats the market by ignoring its ups and downs while continuing to invest.

DOW JONES INDUSTRIAL AVERAGE

Based on the prices of 30 top blue-chip stocks, this index is the most popular, but has not been the most reliable over the past 10 or 15 years because of the increased number of smaller companies. What happens to small companies often has little to do with performance by the Dow's blue chips.

EQUITY (See STOCK and OWNER)

Ownership interest in a corporation in the form of common stock or preferred stock.

FINANCIAL PLANNER

A financial expert who helps you get organized, identifies your goals, and helps you move from your current position toward your financial goals.

FINANCIAL PLANNING

The ongoing creation, implementation and updating of a financial road map designed to get you from where you are to where you want to be.

FINANCIAL SPEED

The rate at which your investments must grow to accumulate the amount needed to fund your objective.

NOTE: Use caution: there is danger in speeding

HARD ASSETS (See COLLECTIBLES)

JUNK BONDS (See MUTUAL FUNDS: Bonds: High-"Yield" Funds)

LIQUIDITY

How available is your capital? Liquidity is the degree of ready access to your money.

LOANER

A term informally used to describe a bondholder—one who "loans" his or her money to a corporation or government entity. One who gives loans to others for the use of his or her money for a period of time and for a fixed rate of interest. This may be done through: annuities; government and corporate bonds; cash surrender value of life insurance; certificate of deposit; checking account; federal agency obligations (Federal, National Mortgage Association, Government National Mortgage Association); loans receivable; money market mutual funds; passbook savings or credit union; or Treasury bills or notes. The purpose is safety of principal and income; but there could be purchasing power, interest rate and business risks.

MARGIN, BUYING ON

When you buy stocks on margin, you pay only a portion of the cost of the stock and borrow the balance from your broker. This option gives you leverage that works in both directions. You only pay a percentage of the purchase price, and the risk of loss is multiplied, as is the possibility of gain.

MARKET CYCLE

The time it takes to go from a high point to a low point to a subsequent high—typically three to five years.

MARKET TIMING (OF MUTUAL FUNDS)

A strategy or process based upon various economic and market indicators that switch an investor's money from the mutual fund (stock or bond) to its companion in a money market fund. Timing is an attempt to avoid market downturns, minimize losses and maximize gains.

MONEY SUPPLY (M-I)

All currency in circulation plus all checking accounts are designated as M-l. Economic theory says that when more money is chasing the same quantities of goods and services, prices are driven up by the pressure of demand; conversely, when the M-l remains steady or drops, prices do likewise.

MONEY MARKET FUNDS

A type of savings account with a depository institution. The federal government insures both principal and interest up to $100,000 per person at one institution.

MUTUAL FUND

A mutual fund pools the small investments of a number of people who have similar objectives. That money is invested in a wide range of securities by a full-time, professional investment manager. Each person who invests in a fund owns part of the portfolio. How big that part is depends upon the total value of the securities in the portfolio. Investors receive their proportionate amount of all the earnings from the securities in the portfolio. Mutual funds offer small investors the same advantages that large investors receive: diversification, lower transaction costs (because the fund can buy securities in big blocks), and full-time professional management. Mutual funds were developed to offer average people a way to invest like the wealthy. If a person has only a few hundred or a few thousand dollars to invest, the investments cannot be so diversified. Millionaires can afford a broadly diversified portfolio to reduce risks and can pay the high fees of the finest advisers to manage the portfolio day by day, selling and buying at the most appropriate times. A millionaire trading in huge lots can get a discounted commission. The mutual fund concept has proved so successful that now millionaires and huge corporations invest in them as well, partly because it is much easier to let a fund manager handle all the bothersome details of buying, selling, record-keeping, and holding the securities in a safe place

MUTUAL FUNDS – BONDS

Corporate bond funds: These are income funds with special emphasis on preservation of principal through a conservative investment policy. As their name implies, they invest primarily in corporate bonds.

GNMA funds: These funds hold mostly Government National Mortgage Association securities (Ginnie Maes). They return principal and interest on a fixed payment schedule.

Government Funds: These funds hold bonds issued by the Treasury and various government agencies.

HIGH-GRADE or Investment-grade corporate bond funds: These funds invest in bonds rated "A" or higher by Standard & Poor's or Moody's Investor Service.

Municipal bond funds: These bonds are designed for people with high incomes who are looking for earnings that will not push them into a higher tax bracket. They invest in municipal bonds, which pay interest that is free from federal income tax. While these funds generally have a lower rate of return than taxable income funds for the person in the higher tax brackets, the after-tax return often can work out to be actually higher.

MUTUAL FUNDS – MONEY MARKET

Money market funds (also called cash reserve): Shares of these funds can be redeemed any time without penalty. They offer the ultimate in liquidity, an option that allows an investor to write checks (usually for $500 or more) and continue to earn dividends until the checks clear. Money market funds generally invest in money instruments such as large certificates of deposits from banks, U.S. government obligations, and major corporate IOUs (short-term commercial paper) with top quality ratings.

Government money market funds: These are the most secure type of money market fund. Though fund shares themselves are not insured, the portfolio is invested solely in short-term securities issued or guaranteed as to principal and interest by the U.S government, its agencies or instrumentalities. Like all money market funds, the objective is highest current income with no penalty for withdrawal, yet with a premium on security, which can mean a slightly lower yield.

Tax-exempt money market funds: Like that of all money market funds, the objective is high current income with no penalty for withdrawal. In these funds, income is exempt from federal income tax. Like regular money market funds, these funds often have check-writing for ultimate liquidity and short portfolio maturity for stability of principal. The primary investment vehicles for tax-free money funds are various short-term municipal bonds.

MUTUAL FUNDS – STOCKS

Growth funds: The primary objective for this type of fund is long-term growth of capital. In other words, increase the value of actual cash outlay over the years. These funds generally do not seek current income, and if they pay any income (dividends), it is likely to be minimal. Growth funds invest principally in common stock. Their objective is to "uncover" growth stocks before they become generally known to the broad investment community and to buy them while they are still undervalued.

Income/growth funds (balanced): The primary objective of these funds is the highest possible current income without undue risk to the principal. Many of these funds also seek a total-rate-of-return. What that means is that, through a flexible asset mix, these funds try to combine capital appreciation and dividends for a stable long-term performance. They invest in bonds convertible to stocks and short-term paper as well as common stocks in high-rated companies.

NASDAQ

An American stock exchange. NASDAQ originally stood for National Association of Securities Dealers Automated Quotations. It is the second-largest stock exchange by market capitalization in the world, after the New York Stock Exchange.

OWNER

One who owns an asset. Assets are characterized by their variable growth, i.e., the ability to increase or decrease in value. The objective of ownership is to grow principal and to fight inflation. Assets can take the form of stocks; real estate; limited partnerships such as real estate, energy or equipment leasing; and/or investment-grade tangible assets such as rare coins, precious metals or collectibles. Risks of ownership are business risk, market risk and liquidity risk.

PRIME RATE

The interest rate major banks charge on short-term loans to their most credit-worthy customers. The government adjusts the prime rate to help stimulate the economy.

PRINCIPAL (See CAPITAL)

PROSPECTUS

Important reading! It is a legal document used to offer a new issue of securities to the public. It describes a company's investments, objectives, policies, services, officers, directors, restrictions, financial statements, charges, and other pertinent information. A publicly traded company is legally required to publish a prospectus.

PURCHASING POWER

The value of the dollar in terms of the goods and services it can buy. As the consumer price index rises, purchasing power declines.

REAL RATE OF RETURN

The accumulated value after subtracting taxes and inflation.

REAL ESTATE INVESTMENT TRUSTS (REITS)

Trusts designed for people or entities that may not meet all the financial requirements or that may not choose to invest a larger amount of money in a less-liquid limited partnership. Developed for individuals and retirement plans that want to invest small amounts of money in the profit potentials that real estate investing offers, but that also want to maintain the liquidity of a stock. An REIT receives money (like a mutual fund) and acquires and holds income properties of all types (industrial, residential, commercial), yet its shares are publicly traded (on the exchanges and over the counter). Distributions may be partially or wholly tax-sheltered, but net operating losses cannot be passed through to an investor to be used to shelter income from other sources—as can occur in a limited partnership.

RISK

Uncertainty. There are five kinds of risk: purchasing power risk; market risk; interest rate risk; liquidity risk and event risk.

RISK MANAGEMENT

The identification and management of those areas or events that may disrupt or destroy various financial goals. Areas of exposure: accident, fire, physical disability, death and mental incapacity. Owing an insurance policy is one example of risk management.

RULE OF 72

Gives you the answer to the question of how long it will take to double your money—for example, to make $1 become $2 at various rates of return. To apply this rule, simply divide the rate of return into 72. Here's a table to help you:

Interest Rate	Rule of 72	Years to Double Money
5 Percent	÷72	14.4
6 Percent	÷72	12
7 Percent	÷72	10.2
8 Percent	÷72	9

SAFETY (OF ONE'S MONEY)

The ability to purchase as many goods and services in the future as you can today.

STOCK

A security representing a portion of ownership in a corporation. Stockholders buy direct ownership in a corporation. Performance of the investment depends on the success or failure of the company. Thus, stocks are called variable-dollar investments because there is no predetermined return.

Common stock: Holders of common stock have the greatest control over the management of the company, but the last claim on its earnings and assets, and therein lies the risk. However, after the fixed claims of the bondholders and preferred stockholders have been met, common stockholders are entitled to share in all the company's further earnings (i.e. dividends).

Preferred stock: A stock that is nonvoting (has no control over the management of the company), but on which a fixed dividend must be paid before holders of common stock is entitled to a dividend each year.

NOTE: "Preferred" does not mean better. Unless it is convertible, it has neither the growth potential of a common stock nor the relative stability of a bond.

TANGIBLES (See COLLECTIBLES)

TIMING (See MARKET TIMING)

TREASURY BILLS (See T-BILLS)

These are short-term and highly liquid. In essence, you are loaning Uncle Sam your money for a short while; he is paying you a rate that reflects what the marketplace is paying during each seven-day period. T-bills come in maturities of three, six and 12 months. They are available in a minimum denomination of $10,000 and in multiples of $5,000 above that. T-bills are sold at a discount from their face value and redeemed (cashed in) at full face value when they mature. Used for safely parking cash.

NOTE: Interest on T-bills is subject to federal income tax but exempt from state and local taxes. To avoid sales charges purchase from Federal Reserve banks or branches.

TREASURY BONDS

Have maturities of five to 30 years, and some are available in $500 denominations. Interest is paid semi-annually and is exempt from state and local taxes.

TREASURY NOTES

Notes are medium-term. They mature anywhere from one to seven years and can be purchased in $1,000 denominations and up. Interest is paid semi-annually and is exempt from state and local taxes.

UNIT TRUSTS

Similar to mutual funds, but the primary difference is the result of the structure of underlying portfolios: A mutual fund is managed full time. The manager has the option to buy, sell, or hold bonds in the portfolio to adapt to changing conditions or implement a change in strategy. A unit trust, on the other hand, is not actively managed. Trust sponsors buy mostly long-term bonds and hold them until maturity, unless they see a default. Even when they cash in their bonds, they do not add new ones.

VOLATILITY

The speed at which the market moves up and down.

YIELD

Income received on investments. It is usually expressed as a percentage of the market price of the security. It is calculated by dividing the fixed annual interest payment by the bond's price (market value).

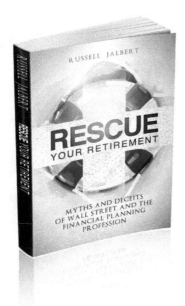

How can you use this book?

MOTIVATE

EDUCATE

THANK

INSPIRE

PROMOTE

CONNECT

Why have a custom version of *Rescue Your Retirement?*

- Build personal bonds with customers, prospects, employees, donors, and key constituencies
- Develop a long-lasting reminder of your event, milestone, or celebration
- Provide a keepsake that inspires change in behavior and change in lives
- Deliver the ultimate "thank you" gift that remains on coffee tables and bookshelves
- Generate the "wow" factor

Books are thoughtful gifts that provide a genuine sentiment that other promotional items cannot express. They promote employee discussions and interaction, reinforce an event's meaning or location, and they make a lasting impression. Use your book to say "Thank You" and show people that you care.